AF521919

Our Town on the Plains

DRVGS &
TOILET ARTICLES
DRUGS

Our Town on the Plains

J. J. PENNELL'S PHOTOGRAPHS OF JUNCTION CITY, KANSAS, 1893–1922

James R. Shortridge

With an essay by John Pultz

UNIVERSITY PRESS OF KANSAS

© 2000 by the University Press of Kansas
Photographs © Spencer Research Library, University of Kansas
All rights reserved

Published by the University Press of Kansas (Lawrence, Kansas 66049), which was organized by the Kansas Board of Regents and is operated and funded by Emporia State University, Fort Hays State University, Kansas State University, Pittsburg State University, the University of Kansas, and Wichita State University.

Library of Congress Cataloging-in-Publication Data

Shortridge, James R., 1944–
Our town on the Plains : J.J. Pennell's photographs of Junction City, Kansas, 1893–1922 / James R. Shortridge ; with an essay by John Pultz.
p. cm.
Includes bibliographical references and index.
ISBN 0-7006-1043-X (alk. paper)
1. Junction City (Kan.)—History—19th century—Pictorial works. 2. Junction City (Kan.)—History—20th century—Sources. I. Pennell, Joseph Judd, 1866–1922. II. Title.

F689.J8 S56 2000
978.1'29—dc21

00-038224

British Library Cataloguing in Publication Data is available.

Printed in Hong Kong by C&C Offset Printing Co., Ltd.
10 9 8 7 6 5 4 3 2 1

The paper used in this publication meets the minimum requirements of the American National Standard for Permanence of Paper for Printed Library Materials Z39.48-1984. ∞

For Garnett and Bob Shortridge,
owners of "reliable and dependable" drugstores
for over seventy years and full participants in the
community life of small-town America

Contents

Maps and Tables

Acknowledgments

The possibility of this book's existence began with the realization by Joseph Stanley Pennell that his father's extensive collection of glass negatives was worth preserving. The University of Kansas Libraries accepted his gift almost one-half century ago, and Professor Robert Taft, photo archivist Nicolette Bromberg, and others at the university have since invested many hours in classification, printmaking, and basic research. I profited greatly from their work. Sheryl Williams, curator of the Kansas Collection in the Spencer Research Library at the university, arranged for the purchase of the *Junction City Union* on microfilm and provided other courtesies that made my research easier. Kristin Eshelman, photo archivist at the Kansas Collection, acted as my primary guide to the Pennell materials and answered a thousand questions with skill and good humor. I also want to thank Sheryl, Kristin, and the rest of the staff at the Kansas Collection for creating a working atmosphere that was at once pleasant and efficient (they even invited me to lunch).

The transformation of Joseph Pennell's heritage into a book began with a generous offer of financial support from Mary Liz Montgomery and from Sue Ann and John G. Montgomery of Junction City for the conversion of the old glass negatives into quality prints. Their support, with that of other donors from Geary County—Myrtle M. Fuller; Arnold Gfeller & Co.; Lee Hornbaker; Jacobson & Jacobson, Attorneys; Chris Rolfs Munson; Marcia L. Plankinton; Edward J. Rolfs; A. J. Sajo; and Robert G. and Betty Rolfs Waters—gave this book its impetus. William Crowe and Keith Russell, the former and present deans, respectively, of the University of Kansas Libraries, provided additional financial support for travel and research assistance, and Fred Woodward at the University Press of Kansas conceived the general format and recruited me as author. During the process of discovery, I was aided by several individuals. In Junction City, Gaylynn Childs, director of the Geary County Historical Museum, answered questions and generously opened her files for my use. John G. Montgomery provided names of contacts, and Mary Liz Montgomery shared her memories of the later Pennell years. She also put me in communication with former resident David Rockwell, another helpful and extremely knowledgeable person about Junction City in the 1910s and early 1920s. A younger native, Shawna Wright, took me on my first tour of the city and discussed her memories of life there a decade ago.

Outside Junction City, time spent looking at Pennell prints with my father, Bob Shortridge, produced much insight into the products, machines, and concerns of that period. Brent Piepergerdes and John Teeple, graduate students in geography and my research assistants on this project, must have had their strangest summer ever. They jumped from the study of laundry machines to that of macadamized roads, and from the history of patent medicines to that of military artillery. All their reports were first class. Beyond this, I want to acknowledge Jon Blumb, who skillfully created all the photographic prints reproduced on the following pages except photos 9, 62, and 77, which were reproduced from prints made by Robert Taft in the 1950s; Darin Grauberger, who drafted quality maps from my sketches; and Marion Bond at the Kansas State Historical Society, who pointed me to the best microfilm readers. Finally, Barbara Shortridge deserves special mention. Although very busy herself in 1999, she made time to provide assistance on research trips and to edit the entire manuscript.

Our Town on the Plains

Joseph Judd Pennell and the Era of Commercial Studio Photography

by John Pultz

From 1888 to 1922, Joseph Judd Pennell worked as a commercial studio photographer in Junction City, Kansas. During his professional life, Pennell produced some 30,000 glass-plate negatives. For about 10 percent of these pictures, Pennell stepped outside the studio, pointing one of his cameras at aspects of life in Junction City. It is these pictures that are the subject of this book. They provide an incredible window onto small-town life in the years around 1900. But Pennell was first and foremost a portraitist who produced exquisite likenesses of town residents and of soldiers stationed nearby at Fort Riley. In this essay, I introduce the person who made both types of photographs, discussing his career as a commercial studio photographer, his place in the history of photography, and the importance of the work.

By good fortune, Pennell worked during the heyday of commercial studio photography in the United States, which had started in 1881. New technology allowed him, like contemporaries elsewhere, to support himself through the production and sale of photographic prints, primarily on a local level. This rooted Pennell culturally and economically in the life of the town and gave his work a visible sense of purpose, utility, and importance for his fellow townspeople. The new technology also made it possible for him to record subjects not previously photographed, in the process endowing Junction City with a palpable and visual coherence that only a medium as persistent and as pervasive as photography can give.

Stemming from this social rootedness, and from the photographer's earnest engagement with his equipment and its traditions, Pennell's photographs were of a generally high quality, marked by good composition, careful lighting, and the rendering of the full range of photographic tones, from light to dark, which gave the forms represented a sense of solidity and three dimensionality. Despite the encroaching inroads of snapshot photography, Pennell and other cameramen were still called upon to record and commemorate life's monuments and transitions. Through their status as professionals and the seeming stability of their pictures, these photographers conferred respectability on middle-class families, including the newly born and the newly dead, and on their homes and businesses.

It was only after Pennell's death in 1922 that this heyday ended. Beginning in the later 1920s and continuing in the 1930s, commercial studio photographers lost their high cultural and economic status, as they yielded their collective ability to create convincing images of middle-class cohesion and stability to snapshot photography and to photographs reproduced in mass-circulation magazines. Ambitious photographers found it more lucrative to sell reproduction rights to their pictures, for publication on the printed page, than to sell actual photographic prints.

The photographs Pennell made seem to be the product of a transcendent, disembodied eye that silently traversed Junction City, chronicling the town's triumphs and defeats, with little trace of its own presence. Depicting objects and images dispersed throughout the town and beyond, they created a bond within the community and gave physical form to assumptions held by many of its citizens, investing their world with a level of detailed information and a three-dimensional solidity that has come to be synonymous with it. As archived in the Kansas Collection of the University of Kansas Libraries, the photographs constitute an important collection, formidable in scope, size, and quality, preserving and cataloging nearly the entire product of the studio (once a shelf in the studio fell, destroying a box of negatives of family subjects). For later eyes, they suggest a world of solid and unquestioned values, caught up in the throes of material things and empirical observation.

Pennell's Life

Pennell was born in King's Creek, North Carolina, on March 9, 1866, a year after the Civil War ended. He was the firstborn of five children. His father, a carpenter whose business had failed, moved the family to Kansas in search of good schools in 1884 or 1885, when the future photographer was in his late teens.[1] Once in Kansas, Joseph Pennell worked in a variety of trades, but primarily as a carpenter, until he found his calling in photography. Family lore suggests several stories that explain this choice. The photographer's son remembers a maternal aunt recalling that after his father had seen a photographic print come up in the developer, he was hooked on making pictures.[2]

Pennell went through a series of partnerships with other photographers before establishing himself in business alone in Junction City. According to a laudatory article entitled "His Splendid Success" that appeared in the *Junction City Sentinel* in 1901, Pennell took a "large stock of energy and ten dollars" and bought half interest in the studio of L. A. Ramsour in March 1888.[3] The business of Ramsour & Pennell, which was on the second floor of the Clark building, flourished, especially with trade that the new partner built up from the nearby military installation at Fort Riley. After a year, Pennell left this partnership to set up a portable darkroom and traveled in the surrounding countryside making photographs for hire. Wanting more stability, he settled back in Junction City the next year and joined with S. D. Hopkins in a studio at Seventh and Franklin. Another year later, Pennell abandoned this partnership for one with Ed Zellner, with whom he worked for two years. Then in 1893 Pennell bought Zellner out and continued in the same location, at 701 North Washington, as the sole proprietor of the business.

In the years that followed, Pennell married and raised a family, developed his business, and became a successful member of the Junction City community. In 1898 he wed Edith Stanley, and in 1901 he built a house for his own family and one next door for her parents (see fig. 76). Two years later his son, Joseph Stanley Pennell, was born. Over the years he joined various clubs in town, including the Rotary and the Chamber of Commerce. He was a member of the Universalist church and active in Freemasonry as a Knight Templar. At his death on April 3, 1922, he was described in one obituary as "prominent in Masonic circles, active in affairs of the city in a civic way, and recognized as a successful man in every way."[4] Another obituary appeared under the headline "Well Known Junction City Business Man Passes Away" and emphasized first the subject's prominence in business and only later mentioned his specific trade, noting that he was "regarded as one of the best photographers in Kansas." In all, it said, he was a "progressive and enterprising business man, a town booster and a man whose loss will be keenly felt."[5]

By the time of the 1901 profile in the *Junction City Sentinel,* Pennell had "acquired the reputation of being a natural artist" and found himself "well and favorably known throughout the state." He had "one of the best equipped galleries in Kansas" and "a business that is equalled by few studios in the west." Over the previous six years, the *Sentinel* continued, he had won medals for "artistic and excellent work," and his pictures had been published in leading photographic journals and popular magazines, including *Munsey's, Ladies' Home Journal,* and *Truth.*

By 1908, Pennell's studio was preeminent among the three photography businesses in Junction City.[6] His studio had two telephones and employed an office boy, a photographer, a retoucher, and an apprentice.[7] Later that year, he built a building at 801 North Washington for his studio and received praise for his foresight in moving the business district a block north. The staff and new space were in keeping with the studio's prodigious production. In 1908 the studio produced between 1,600 and 1,800 negatives, or almost one an hour throughout the year. (More commonly, the studio produced 1,000 to 1,400 negatives a year.)

Like many other businessmen in town, Pennell prospered from the reliable infusion of money into the Junction City economy from the nearby military installation. Indications of Pennell's prosperity and status can be seen not just in the number of photographs made or the size of his staff but also in the portraits he made of himself and with his wife and son. The elder Pennell appears as a serious, sober, bourgeois man, pleased with himself and his upward mobility, always carefully and formally dressed and never smiling. His own ability to put his subjects and their needs first is suggested in one of these family portraits. Pennell stands to the side, leaving at center stage his wife, who looks with self-assured confidence into the camera, apparently trustful that her husband will present her most subtle inner self (fig. 1). The only photographs that suggest a lighter side to the photographer show him with a guitar and, later in his life, with golf clubs.

1. Joseph and Edith Pennell, 1899 (print 394.1). Pennell made this portrait of himself with his wife a year after their marriage and four years before the birth of their son. Although props and illusionistic backgrounds are absent, the strong interplay of light and shadow elevates this portrait into a seemingly timeless and idealized realm.

Pennell's economic and social status might also be judged from that of his clients. Many of Junction City's most successful merchants turned to Pennell when they wanted photographs that would not only record but also mark as special their families, their houses, and their stores. The pictures that resulted suggest that Pennell identified closely with his well-to-do clients. In them, he appears to have collaborated with his clients in a celebration of physical things and material success.

Pennell's Portraits

Portraiture was the centerpiece of Pennell's practice and took many forms. Uniformed soldiers, farmers with tools, beautiful young women, successful businessmen, couples, mothers and sons, women with their sisters, men with their buddies, parents with babies and growing children, African Americans, Mexican Americans, and Euro-Americans all came to the studio and posed, standing and seated, for head-and-shoulder, three-quarter, and full-figure views. It is clear from the evidence of his work why he was so popular and successful. The portraits are charming and elegant and instill in the subjects character and culture. By bathing them in soft but directional lighting and coaxing calm expressions, Pennell made his subjects handsome and beautiful, dignified and wise.

Pennell wanted his portraits to be distinct from snapshots, which were becoming popular at the time, and they were. Through a variety of means, he ensured that the likenesses he produced possessed a grandeur and dignity absent from the more casual and spontaneous interlopers. To endow his portraits with allusions to transcendence, beauty, culture, and history, he employed various props and backdrops. Props included a heavily carved chair that was suggestive of the Renaissance. One backdrop included columns and heavy curtains in the manner of Titian and Van Dyck, to evoke culture and the classical past (see fig. 104). Several others evoked the natural world so prized by the nineteenth-century Romantic tradition. Several showed trees, near and far, against cloud-dappled skies (see fig. 39); another showed a curving shoreline and distant lighthouse (see fig. 101). To make this latter backdrop seem even more real, Pennell would sometimes use with it a floor covering that looked like seaweed.

The moods of the portraits vary, presumably to fit the wishes and character of the sitters. Some are very formal, even stiff, like the one of Pennell with his wife. Others are more playful. A group portrait from 1899 shows two young couples exploiting the shoreline backdrop to put themselves at the beach, sporting umbrellas to protect themselves from the fictional sun's rays (fig. 2). In another case, two couples had themselves photographed in the studio, playing cards at a table.

The style of Pennell's portraits changed over time. In part, this stemmed from the sitters, who in dress, hairstyle, and demeanor comported themselves according to the dictates of contemporary fashion. But this also came from Pennell's own efforts, conscious or not. His portraits of the 1890s are dense and dark, full of late Victorian grandeur and high seriousness. As the years progressed, the tonality lightened and the space of the pictures became simpler, as is evident in a comparison of figure 31, from 1900, with figures 145 and 146, made in 1908 and

2. Purcell group, 1899 (print 395). Rakish frivolity dominates this clever group portrait, posed before a painted backdrop. Its edges, which we see most clearly on the right and in the foreground, would have been cropped from the finished print.

1922, respectively. Stylistic changes can be seen in the studio props and backdrops that appear and disappear over time. By 1909, Pennell had introduced an adjustable wooden column on which his clients could lean, forswearing the more formal and erect poses of a decade earlier. By the early 1920s, he had added a new backdrop, with open latticework framing a clean white field. Gone are the references to the seaside or to the classical past, replaced by the simplicity of a Japanese-inspired modernism.

To distinguish his work from snapshot photography and meet his clients' needs and desires for prints of various sizes, Pennell used plates in a range of formats (4×5 inch, 5×7 inch, 6×9 inch, 8×10 inch, 11×14 inch, 12×20 inch, and even panoramic negatives that were some 30 inches wide), although most of his work was done in 5×7 and 8×10 formats. Pennell seldom varied the negative size to fit his subjects. He used 11×14 negatives to photograph single figures as well as groups of eight or more. He did, however, reserve 4×5 negatives for more humble undertakings. These were often less formal, less artistically rendered portraits that were closer to simple head-and-shoulder shots. Frequently Pennell would go even further, dividing a 4×5-inch negative to produce two, three, four, or even six small images on the same plate. That the larger negatives dominate in the Pennell collection reminds us that his was a high-class operation, with most portraits being more than mere identity cards. Pennell seems not to have followed the advice, given in 1912, that studio photographers should offer different grades of portraits, including "a style of picture which was not cheap looking and at the same time not expensive . . . something attractive and at the same time different from [their] high grade work."[8]

Larger-size plates were easier to retouch, which was another way that studio photographers could distinguish their work from snapshot photography. Nearly all Pennell's pictures show retouching in the flesh of the face and hands. This was done to render these areas as broad middle grays without the specificity of precise skin texture. One exception is a 1923 portrait (made by the studio after Pennell's death) of a young girl, Betty Hamilton, whose skin was left unretouched to reveal her freckles. Retouching also weakened or obscured lines and wrinkles, which, when done well, would certainly have endeared the photographer to his client. Retouching for the most part consisted of small comma-shaped strokes applied to the emulsion side of the negative, with additional highlighting of the pupils of the eyes. Such work was tedious, and for most of his career, Pennell employed a retoucher in addition to other assistants.

Once the negatives were finished, Pennell or an assistant would put a strip of opaque tape along one edge and write on it the name of the sitter and often the details of the order (for example, "six of each/1.50"). Pennell also kept logbooks, into which he entered basic data on each order. These books, totaling ten in number, are the sources for the estimates of Pennell's yearly output. The prints themselves were mounted on sheets of cardboard tinted to elegant browns and grays or were placed in fine-paper folders. For pictures that were to be sold in quantity, such as scenes at Fort Riley, Pennell would label and sign them by writing on the negatives in reverse with opaque ink. For portraits, his signature took the form of one of several metal dies with which he would emboss the cardstock or, at times, the form of a gold-tone seal.

Pennell invested his artistic ambition in his portraiture. A member and sometimes an officer of state and national photography organizations, he submitted his portraits to the competitions they ran and frequently won prizes. He participated in photography exhibitions held at the World's Columbian Exposition in Chicago in 1893 and at the Louisiana Purchase Exposition in Saint Louis in 1904.[9] In 1905, he entered six large photographs in the class A competition at the Kansas Photographers' Association convention in Wichita, where they were judged according to lighting, poses, chemical effect, and general effect. One of his pictures, a portrait of Lucy M. Keeshan, won first prize as best in the state.[10] It also won a prize from the Eastman Kodak Company in its first national competition.[11]

Pennell's portraits of Keeshan (he made several; which one won the prize we do not know) are representative of his work but hardly exceptional. Keeshan appears in one standing in a long dress, hands together, before a painted column; in another she is seated before a plain background. More artistically ambitious is his portrait of Mildred Mullis from 1899 (fig. 3). It shows a long-haired girl, flower in hand, languorously leaning her head into a full-length mirror, which reflects back the image of this girl. The mirror as a device in Victorian photographic portraiture occurs most famously in the pictures of girls and young women made in the 1860s by Lady Hawarden, an early British pictorialist. The mirror suggests the solipsistic innocence of a young girl, her beauty directed internally, only at herself, not toward the suitors who only a few years later will be central to her life. Thus the mirror conjures innocence and inwardness. The mirror, furthermore, can be said to represent the process of photography itself.

Even more artistically ambitious, although not a portrait, is Pennell's *Robbing the Male,* from 1906 to 1908. A mini-drama staged and photographed in his studio (as the familiar backdrops reveal), it shows a white-gowned woman stealing money from the pants hanging at the bedside of a sleeping man. This picture was an invented narrative, a type of image that had interested ambitious photographers since the 1850s. It is very close in theme and composition to a stereograph by the Philadelphia photographer William H. Rau, entitled *Robbing the (Male) Mail,* which was published in 1895 by Griffith & Griffith of Philadelphia, Saint Louis, and Liverpool. That this theme existed in Rau's stereograph prior to Pennell's version reminds us of the Kansan's connection to photography and photographers beyond the limits of Junction City, if in no other way than through the traffic in photographs themselves. Even more notable, from our perspective, is that Pennell's photograph of this theme is more artistically rendered than Rau's, with far more subtle use of lighting, pose, expression, and props. That Rau, like Pennell, is better known for his documentary photography (he was the official photographer of the Pennsylvania and Lehigh Valley Railroads) is witness to the complex makeup of commercial photography practice in the years around 1900 and the range of work undertaken by a single practitioner.

3 (opposite). Mildred Mullis, 1899 (print 433.1). One of Pennell's most romantic portraits, this picture uses the mirror and flower to suggest girlhood innocence. The mirror also creates delightful complexity at the center of the image.

The "Dry-Plate" Revolution and Photography on Location

For the thirty years before Pennell took up photography, it had been dominated by the collodion (or "wet-plate") process, which required photographers to make their exposures when the photosensitive emulsion they had coated onto plate glass was still wet.[12] As a consequence, photographers either had to work close to their darkrooms or had to bring a darkroom with them to any remote subject. By 1881, George Eastman had perfected and industrialized a process whereby glass plates could be coated with silver salts embedded in gelatin and allowed to dry in advance of use. As a result of this, photographers could buy ready-to-use negatives from national suppliers, which freed them from their role as chemists and from the tether of the darkroom. At the same time, gelatin replaced albumen as the binding agent in the production of photographic papers. The combination of dry-plate negatives and gelatin-silver prints gave a tremendous boost to photography and created the era when photographers could earn reasonable incomes and social status through the sale of pictures themselves. The decade of the 1880s saw the number of photographers in the United States increase at a rate four times that of the general population.[13] Dry-plate methods made photography cheaper and more accessible, especially beyond the confines of the studio itself. And because dry-plate negatives were purchased ready-made, they ended the earlier practice of photographers' cleaning off and reusing their plates, which effectively prevented the accumulation of the sort of visual archive Pennell achieved.

The freedom to photograph away from the studio or a darkroom had little effect on Pennell's portrait practice. It did, however, make possible the rest of his work. The difficulty and expense of the wet-plate process had meant that only subjects of interest to a great many people, or ones with wealth or power, were likely to be photographed. For instance, the Civil War and the American West were of interest to all Americans and became classic subjects of wet-plate photography, the former in the work of Mathew Brady and his assistants, and the latter in the work of Timothy H. O'Sullivan and other expeditionary photographers. The ability to photograph away from a darkroom made it feasible, in technical and economic terms, to take photographs that were of interest to far fewer people. In the case of Pennell, this might mean as few viewers as the population of Junction City or one's friends and family.

Consequently, the pictures in this book, especially those dating from the 1890s and the first decade of the twentieth century, were novelties. In commissioning Pennell to photograph this house or that business, Junction City residents were obtaining new sorts of images, with no real predecessors. The finished pictures themselves, in their content, form, and variety, testify to photographic innovation and to the era's fascination with what new photographic technology made possible. One senses in the decision to commission photographs, and in the making and the viewing of them, a delight in subjecting varied aspects of life to this new medium. These photographs also gave people images of themselves and their community that they had not previously had. For the first time, residents could possess images that marked out their town, becoming a virtual surrogate for it, making literal and visual the hierarchy of what was important. This process reified or gave physical and visual form to a series of civic relationships among residents and between residents and the town itself that were real but had previously had no visual representation.

When Pennell left the studio to photograph, he did so to make pictures he thought he could sell or ones for which he had been commissioned. Pictures he made to sell on speculation included those of encampments at Fort Riley, which he labeled in the negatives and would sell to soldiers passing through; of the May 1903 flood (see fig. 114); and even of the road connecting Junction City and the fort (see fig. 54). The last of these also appeared as a postcard printed in Germany and published by R. O. Thomen of Junction City.[14] Fort Riley pictures were also published in J. J. Pennell and C. S. McGinn's *Picturesque Fort Riley* (1900) and, according to Joseph Stanley Pennell, in *The Rasp,* the Fort Riley yearbook.[15]

Among the commissioned pictures are many that represented the town's economic life, showing new businesses, new buildings built to house those new businesses, the store windows of the businesses, and equipment used in the businesses (a hearse, trucks, and trains). It is in these pictures that Pennell's own status as a businessman and a member of the business community is most evident. That these pictures were made, and made this well, gives visual form to the mercantile values shared by many in Junction City. These pictures endow commerce with the appearance of dignity and stability. Pennell worked hard and produced excellent pictures in all these categories. Especially noticeable are the pictures of store windows, which are carefully set up to avoid reflections and remain elegant but simple, and those of store interiors, which required that Pennell find the right vantage point, choose the right lens, and adjust the light so that he could include as much of the interior space as possible and still retain vivid detail. The amount of effort that Pennell put into these pictures attests to his devotion to his craft and to his desire—even after he was successful—to put himself fully into his work, finding a unique solution for each commission.

Another category of pictures, most of which were presumably commissioned or for sale, shows people and events and includes parades and unveilings, celebratory dinners and parties, school groups (clubs, classes, drama troupes, and sporting teams), and other groups, such as clubs, bands, and troops. Most notable in these pictures is Pennell's repeated ability to capture each of the group members with eyes open and an engaged visage. For example, in a group picture of the Junction City High School editorial board from 1910, their poses look natural yet choreographed, and the picture is thoughtfully lit, as if it were a scene from a play (fig. 4). The picture is well crafted, creating an image that seems stable and permanent rather than temporary and contingent, thus reifying personal and civic values held in common by the dominant classes of Junction City.

These pictures all take on new life when we remind ourselves of the collaboration that went on between Pennell and the subjects in their making. A client, we should remember, had most often approached Pennell and was paying for the picture. Looking at such pictures,

4. Editorial board, Junction City High School, 1910 (print 2286). These budding writers and journalists appear engaged in a series of activities that suggest the mostly inward and cerebral duties of the high school editorial board: writing, reading, typing, and editing. One of a number of pictures Pennell made for area schools, this one uses careful lighting and posing to produce a unified tableau.

we can sense the excitement of all involved. For the client, there was a desire to have a picture of a particular thing, place, or event. And to have such a picture was likely a novelty for this person, who seems to be engaged in an act of self-presentation in its making.

Pennell made one type of picture over and over, which was to show someone's pride of ownership in a home, a business, or a means of transportation. In making pictures of homes, as he did in photographing other Junction City sites, Pennell collaborated with residents in pointing out what mattered to them and, in the process, helped develop a visual corollary to social and civic ideals. In some pictures, Pennell worked at a distance, rendering each house in its entirety and isolated from its neighbors, as it towered upward and dominated the photographic frame (see figs. 77 and 79). In a variant, the owner posed before the house. In figure 78, family members are spread throughout the front yard, as if to colonize that space and mark the extent of landholdings. Their splendid isolation gives the picture a proto-surrealist air, with unseen attraction and repulsion seeming to determine the figures' positions, not unlike the paintings of Swiss artist Ferdinand Hodler, which similarly showed individuals in strangely isolated spaces. In a further variant, property owners wished to show not just their homes but also the means of transportation they owned, be it merely a horse-drawn wagon (see figs. 42 and 74) or the newly fashionable bicycle (see fig. 128). In figure 42, Pennell's choice of vantage point, down the road from the house itself, allows the inclusion of place-setting details and of more of this farmer's land, the capital upon which his livelihood depends.

Many other pictures define livelihoods. In figure 43, Andrew Engstrom has asked Pennell to document his remarkably tall corn (is this at the edge of the field, or did Pennell have to clear space for his camera and tripod within the field itself, where the corn would be at its tallest?). In figure 44, Thomas Dixon (we presume) poses with the workers, infrastructure, and stock that constitute his stockyards.

Prefiguring the late-twentieth-century vogue for commercial portraits made away from the photographer's studio and within the confines of the subject's home is Pennell's picture of Lieutenant Frank Otis with his wife and three young boys (see fig. 91). Here, Lieutenant Otis appears with his own props, in his own home, where he can display as part of his family's portrait their opulent belongings and good taste. Once we see that the scene has been set up for the camera (chairs have been brought into the room and placed in front of other pieces of furniture), we can observe the family's collaboration with Pennell to give a rich visual representation of their values, which include not only respect for the children but also an appreciation of order, cleanliness, and tasteful material possessions. Pennell's part in this production included the use of a wide-angle lens, which allows the inclusion of a broad scene that takes in three separate arenas of activity as well as carpets, furniture, and other luxury items.

Formally, one of the most salient aspects of Pennell's photography is his wise and careful use of the wide-angle lens.[16] Anyone who has used a standard snapshot camera has experienced how its inability to take in a broad scene often creates a photograph at odds with one's experience. Seldom can one record with satisfaction the spatial extent of a room or of an outdoor scene. One can record events within a room or outside, but the sense of spaciousness of the place itself eludes most cameras. Through the careful use of the wide-angle lens, Pennell made pictures that are masterful in their depiction of space, with the effect that they not only record the event at hand but also give a clear sense of where it took place. By placing events in space and making place itself one of its subjects, Pennell's photography contributed to the town's understanding of itself. This is part of the power the photographs retain, as they conjure up for viewers a century later a sense of Junction City at this earlier time.

One sees this wide space in such images as figure 134, which shows Junction City residents out inspecting a recently crowned road. Pennell's distance from the four figures reminds us that the subject is not them but the road itself, which strangely, surreally heads straight through the middle of the picture, with little variation. The broad angle of view that Pennell has taken opens up the space and includes enough of the adjoining brush to give a real sense of passage. It also subordinates the individuals to larger, civic values, embodied in the care of the road itself.

The End of the Era of Commercial Studio Photography

Soon after Eastman industrialized the production of ready-to-use glass plates, he transferred dry-plate technology to roll film, which he marketed to amateurs in the form of the Kodak snapshot camera. This equipment was so easy to use that Eastman's company could advertise it under the slogan "You press the button; we do the rest." The Kodak first appeared in 1888, the year Pennell began making photographs, but he apparently never saw it as competition. As early as 1896, the ink stamp that Pennell put on some of his pictures advertised that his studio not only provided fine photography but also sold Kodak cameras and processed Kodak film.[17] It appears that Pennell even made several photographs to advertise Kodak cameras.[18] The first, from around 1900, shows one finely dressed woman making a snapshot of another on the bank of a local river. Pennell's vantage point, higher up on the riverbank, places the women's faces in shadow with little definition, while emphasizing their actions. The finished picture is exceptional for its narrative quality: the process of photographing, not the women, becomes the subject. The other picture shows a young boy, Gilbert Emick, at the Smoky Hill River using a Kodak box camera to photograph two friends who hold up for display their catch of fish (fig. 5).

These two pictures document the concurrence of snapshot and professional photography: Pennell, the professional, lugs his bulky view camera out to the riverside to produce negatives that his studio will process and print; his subjects, amateur photographers, use lighter, more easily carried Kodak cameras that they will hand over to others, who will remove, develop, and print the film. These two pictures also remind us that behind all of Pennell's pictures was someone's choice, whether conscious or not, to employ a professional photographer rather than to make a snapshot. Likewise, in several other activities, including shaving and laundry, Junction City residents could choose between performing the activity themselves or having it done outside the house, within the public arena.

5. Gilbert Emick at Smoky Hill River, 1902 (print 871). Two worlds of photography meet in this image: the careful professional work of Pennell and the amateur production of snapshot photography. But even so, all is not what it appears to be. It is unlikely that these boys fished in these outfits. The dictates of studio photography seem to have prevailed, as Emick and his friends have dressed for this special occasion.

6. John Welsh and catfish, 1901 (print 726). Welsh's catch is surely worthy of this photographic record. Pennell used a backdrop that suggests that Welsh and the fish are still outside, not in Pennell's second-story downtown studio.

The nature of this choice is made vivid when we compare the picture we imagine young Emick would have made at the river of his friends and their catch with pictures Pennell made of individuals who came to his studio with fish or fowl, seeking a record of their sportsmanship (fig. 6). In the latter cases, the sportsmen must have returned home from hunting or fishing, put on their best outfits, and headed to Pennell's studio for a formal picture of the prized catch. Years later, such pictures would surely have been done exclusively at home or afield with a snapshot camera. But at this time, even though a snapshot was an option, professional work of the sort Pennell produced was still preferred. In fact, it would not be until the 1920s and 1930s that snapshot photography really took off.

What are the differences between these two options? One is obvious. The trip to Pennell's studio would surely have produced a picture that was more sophisticated technically, formally, and in presentation than the snapshot. Another difference is less obvious, although more important for the social history of photography. Having Pennell make the picture conferred upon the process and the resulting picture something of a ritualistic and public nature. In the simplest sense, it certified that the picture would be good. Having him do it also brought the picture's production into the public realm. Rather than being just an action among the given sportsmen or between a fisherman and his wife, the picture making had a public quality to it. It took place within the public realm, which included trips to Pennell's studio to pose and to pick up the finished print, and the revelation of the desire for such a picture to Pennell and his staff.

With the ascendancy of snapshot photography in the 1930s, this public aspect of photography would be gone, replaced by more isolated and private acts of photography. Closely related to this would be the end of the kind of detailed documentation of each small town that negatives such as Pennell's provide. In the confluence of the style, content, and mode of production found in *Life* and other picture magazines, a national archive of generic small-town life was created. No longer was each small town documented by its own commercial photographers who made the sort of pictures that Pennell made, commissioned and bought by locals. Rather, photographers working for the Farm Security Administration and the magazines produced such pictures on a national scale, obviating the need for each town to have its own cache of pictures that were at once unique and mythically generic. It is perhaps only with the advent of cable television, and its expansion of community access and local coverage, that a means has returned for such a detailed visual rendering of one's own locale.

The Life of Pennell's Negatives After His Death

Following Pennell's death in 1922, his wife ran the studio for another year. Then it appears that someone else took over, and the studio continued to operate under the Pennell name until the 1940s.[19] In 1950, Joseph Stanley Pennell, who had established himself as a writer (when his first novel, *The History of Rome Hanks,* appeared in 1944, some critics called him the most promising writer to emerge in a decade), offered his father's negatives to the University of Kansas.[20] The younger Pennell contacted Robert Taft, a chemistry professor at the university who was interested in photography. Pennell had enjoyed reading Taft's 1938 book

Photography and the American Scene: A Social History 1839–1889, one of the first American histories of photography.[21] That Taft would be interested in Pennell's photography is not surprising, given the attention he devoted to commercial and studio photography in his book. In this emphasis, Taft differed greatly from Beaumont Newhall, a librarian and later curator at the Museum of Modern Art in New York, who also published a history of photography in the late 1930s. Newhall, who had been trained in print connoisseurship at Harvard, wrote a history that showcased the work of modernist photographers but had little interest in commercial and studio photography. Taft took a very different approach to photography. Initially concerned with its technical aspects, he changed his area of interest and set out in his book "to trace, however imperfectly, the effects of photography upon the social history of America, and in turn the effect of social life upon the progress of photography." To do so, he continued, he took as his "outline a discussion of the history (as it affected this country primarily) of the various forms of photographs, each of which in its day has had its turn as the reigning favorite. After all, it is just as important historically to know who and what were photographed, and by whom, as it is to know how the photographing was done."[22]

Taft was the one who retrieved Pennell's negatives from the Junction City studio. He deposited some 30,000 glass plates at the University of Kansas in 1951, where they remain to this day. He proceeded to clean them (in a manner that turns out to have been harmful) and make prints from them. Taft sorted through the negatives and culled for printing 4,212 that matched his list of important subjects: street scenes, agricultural scenes, architecture, businesses or occupations, social gatherings, ceremonies, events, Fort Riley–related images, minorities, and photographs that provided more information on the photographer's work. (Another 400 were printed with the support of a grant from the National Endowment for the Humanities in the early 1980s.[23])

At the time of the donation, Joseph Stanley Pennell had a modest sense of the photographs' value and saw them as a window on American small-town life at the beginning of the twentieth century.[24] He did, though, want the photographs to serve as a memorial to his father. When Taft suggested that only the "desirable" among the portrait negatives might be kept, the photographer's son was agreeable: "A few [of the portraits] would make costume plates (dress uniforms, civilian clothes of the late nineteenth century etc.) but the bulk of them are nothing but Joe or Josephine Doakes and only the preservation of a Big Day in a little life. That's a pretty sad truth."[25] Despite the son's acquiescence, none of the negatives were destroyed or removed from the archive.

The value of Taft's and Pennell's appraisal has been borne out by the use made of the negatives over the years. As they presumed, the photographs that are not portraits have gained the greatest attention. The richness of the collection is suggested by the range of venues in which the images have appeared. They have been reprinted in a number of books about American life, including *An American Album* (American Heritage, 1968), *The Fabulous Century* (Time-Life, 1969), and *The Way Life Was* (Chanticleer Press, 1974), but they have also been used to contribute to much more specialized works: PBS films on baseball and on the American West, a *Life* magazine special issue on the Bill of Rights, a book on the Irish in America, an exhibition of photographs of war organized by the Corcoran Gallery of Art in Washington, D.C., and the opening credits of the television series *Cheers.*

The photographs have been the focus of two one-person exhibitions: *An Exhibition of Photographs 1895–1909 from the J. J. Pennell Collection,* organized by Taft when the work first arrived at the University of Kansas, and *Frozen in Time: J. J. Pennell's Junction City Photographs: 1895–1922,* organized in 1980 by Thomas Southall for the university's Spencer Museum of Art. Taft's exhibition included 300 pictures and was intended to highlight the university's acquisition of the collection and suggest its possible uses by students of military, local, and Kansas history; by students of sociology; and by writers, artists, illustrators, and designers. The exhibition stressed the transformation of Junction City, as seen through the photographs, from the "horse age to the auto age," as Taft wrote for the exhibition brochure. Southall's exhibition gave greater emphasis to Pennell, looking at the man and his production of negatives. Pennell's photographs also formed the centerpiece of a film, *Junction City, 1890–1915,* which was intended as the "focal point of a discussion . . . on the topic of urbanization and technological change in Kansas."[26]

The Sad Loss of the Handcrafted, the Small, and the Local

Pennell's photographs are remarkable documents. They not only stand for life in Junction City but also are testaments to a time when photography was a different sort of profession and photographs had a different cultural meaning than they do today. The photograph in Pennell's era remained a handcrafted object of local origins, even while other aspects of life increasingly gave way to the mass produced, as Pennell himself would document. In the end, we must see Pennell not as an impartial observer of the changes around him but as someone whose profession and means of livelihood were caught up in those changes. Had the photographer lived beyond his mere fifty-six years, the tributes he received at the end of his life might well have been different, the accolades absent. Rather than leaving the world a hero of the business and professional worlds, he could have been, even ten years later, a broken man whose photographic work was no longer needed by a small town whose citizens could instead participate in a larger visual, even virtual community, at the loss, though, of their own real community, as reified in part through Pennell's photographs and the role they played therein.

Junction City in a Golden Age, 1893–1922

On July 10, 1921, when the construction firm of Ziegler and Dalton announced that Geary County now possessed the first border-to-border, hard-surfaced highway in Kansas, Junction City boosters were elated. Their joy was partly because it was a local company that had poured this eighteen-foot slab of concrete, but even more because the town chamber of commerce had just lobbied successfully to make the pavement part of a new interstate route then being marked from Kansas City to Colorado Springs. Later that year, when told that this Golden Belt route was to become a link in the Victory Highway, a truly national thoroughfare, townspeople could hardly contain themselves. Here was proof that the growth and prosperity that had characterized their community for the previous thirty-five years would continue unabated.[1]

Although census figures reveal that the population of Junction City has indeed increased regularly in the years since 1921, these subsequent decades turned out to be considerably less glorious than residents had expected. In fact, the pouring of this first highway can be seen as the end of an era. Despite the growth, residents somehow began to lose their sense of self-importance after that time. Never again would they feel so much in control of their own destiny as they did then. Never again would they see themselves so much as a single, extended family. The period I refer to is not unique to Junction City. Although it has no commonly accepted name, it is widely associated with moderate-sized communities in the Midwest and, to a lesser extent, across the country as a whole. The time varies a little from place to place, but in Junction City it extended from the late 1880s to the early 1920s. What made this time special is hard to discern at first. When the years are examined closely, one sees considerable change, including the seeds of ideas that would yield profound social and economic consequences in the future. Three generations of popular writing about this time largely ignore such developments, however. These books and essays focus instead on a certain stability and optimism about life in those years. They often have a wistful tone, a sense that something good has been lost in the decades since. In their eyes, the turn of the century was a golden age.[2]

To label any period a golden age is an exercise in gross generalization. Certainly 1900 was not an ideal time to be a person of color in Junction City. Nor was it a good time for a child who had contracted diphtheria or influenza or for a young woman who held professional ambitions beyond those of teaching or nursing. Still, even knowing these truths, it is possible to find many things to admire about these decades and even more to be curious about.

Much of the character of that now vanished world—especially its almost defining characteristic of a community closeness juxtaposed with a surprising degree of sophistication—derives from a particular two-tiered transportation system. Railroads were one component, an efficient national network that allowed buyers from local Junction City stores to inspect wholesale houses and factories in Saint Louis and Chicago, children of wealthy citizens to attend college at Wellesley and Stanford, and successful merchants to take hunting trips to the Ozarks and the Rockies. The other primary means of transportation, the horse, counterbalanced this connectivity. Horses implied a tremendously more restricted circle of activity. Travel in a buggy any farther than three or four miles to buy simple perishable goods such as sugar or tobacco made no economic sense. Even the more specialized merchants and manufacturers in Junction City and other substantial communities of its size (about 5,000 people) could not expect to draw Saturday shoppers from farms beyond a twenty-mile radius.[3]

The railroad-horse combination produced a somewhat paradoxical social world. Isolation was still profound in farming areas, especially before the post office initiated its system of free rural delivery in 1902 (1904 for Geary County).[4] Spring rains or winter storms could cancel what were already infrequent trips to town for many women. Conversely, middle-class people in communities fortunate enough to have good rail service and county-seat status could easily feel very good about their position in life. Older citizens regularly recounted the past heroic and successful struggles to attract the initial railroads and the government offices, while current business leaders took every opportunity to tick off long lists of new buildings, steadily growing deposits at the local banks, and civic improvements that ranged from sewers and telephones to opera houses and libraries. People in such places did not feel at all isolated. Quite naturally, they also thought that the prosperity coming their way was primarily the result of their own hard work and progressive thinking. The possibility that the same isolation that limited the activities and choices of rural people was also creating a captive market for their own goods and services was rarely, if ever, voiced.

It is common knowledge that the widespread adoption of the automobile was central to many cultural changes in the twentieth century. What is not often realized, however, is that its most fundamental impacts—reducing social isolation and increasing economic competition among communities—did not begin with the first wave of purchases of the new machines or affect all places at the same rate. Junction City people, for example, acquired their first automobiles in 1905. The accounts in the local newspapers make it clear that they enjoyed the new runabouts and touring cars immensely and that the accompanying loud horns and gasoline pumps changed the look and feel of the town almost immediately. Despite such clamor, however, the economic effects were minimal. Automobiles remained largely playthings for the next ten to fifteen years. When farmers began to buy them in numbers about 1910, it is true that sales in the general stores at Alida, Briggs, Wreford, and other hamlets in

Geary County declined somewhat. Junction City merchants, however, accepted their slightly increased sales volume as part of the general prosperity of the times. Overall, the social and economic feel of the town was much the same in 1920 as it had been in 1890 or even before.

By pure serendipity, the magnificent photographic record produced by Joseph J. Pennell coincides closely with the period I have been describing. The date of his death in April 1922 approximates the dawn of modern, automobile-dominated America. Moreover, his earliest surviving local photographs, from 1893, occur just a few years after Junction City residents learned that their nearby military post, Fort Riley, was to be spared the decommissioning that was the fate of nearly all frontier bases. Instead, General Sheridan had declared that Riley was to become a permanent facility, the principal training center for the U.S. Cavalry. Congressional approval of $750,000 in construction contracts for the years 1886–1891 launched Junction City on an almost giddy period of prosperity.[5] The ensuing decades probably would have been remembered as a golden age in Geary County even without this big infusion of money. With it, the word *golden* takes on additional meaning.

Although Pennell's primary business was making studio portraits, he also found time to record much of the landscape and mood of this heady time. His pictorial account is biased, of course. It reflects only a single perspective and the obvious predilections of his middle-class, probusiness, and Anglo-American male existence. Compared with what survives for other communities, however, it is a wondrously complete legacy. The photographs reproduced on the following pages provide a sampling of his insights. My words try to interpret them and then to add commentary on aspects of the town that escaped his lens.

Junction City Before Pennell

When J. J. Pennell's photographs are reproduced in books and magazines, they usually are intended to illustrate an event, style, or scene typical of the Midwest at the dawn of the twentieth century. For the most part, I use them in this way as well. Readers should know from the outset, however, that Junction City has never been particularly typical of towns its size. This is true whether the comparison is with the United States as a whole, with the Midwest, or even with Kansas. Having Fort Riley three miles away makes local life different in many ways. Junction City, in fact, is a classic military town. The post predates the city by about six years and was the principal reason why urban speculators came here in the first place. The range of town businesses is influenced by the continuing possibility of large military contracts for fuel, for agricultural and manufactured products, and especially for construction. The presence of numerous young soldiers has always affected local social mores and activities. In the early years, the connections were predicted to yield even greater dividends. The same basic set of geographical considerations that had led to the fort's establishment at this site gave hope to the founders of Junction City and to other entrepreneurs that a town adjacent to this post might become considerably more than a simple military supply station. Such grandiose aspirations, and the subsequent disappointments when they failed to materialize, affected the mind-sets of Junction City people. Because of this, a sketch of the early years is necessary background for the Pennell period.

Basic questions for anybody who tries to understand Junction City and the ambitions of its founders are why Fort Riley was established and what strategic role it was expected to fulfill. The context for these issues is the rise of American interests in Santa Fe, Oregon, California, and other sections of the far western portion of the continent during the 1840s and 1850s. This expansion had complex social and economic implications, including a stretching of the financial resources of the U.S. Army. The old concept of a neat line of fortifications that could separate white and Indian settlements along the eastern edge of the Great Plains no longer had validity. Instead, politicians and the public demanded new outposts that could protect migrants and tradesmen in the West. Soon these sprang up, nearly all in remote locations. Fort Laramie along the Oregon Trail and Forts Atkinson and Union on the Santa Fe route were among the most prominent.[6]

The next issue was how to supply the new posts. Steamboats had worked well before the big western expansion, but now the nearest ports were Fort Leavenworth on the Missouri River and Fort Gibson on the Arkansas, both several hundred miles away from the new garrisons. Overland freighting would work, of course, but this was both expensive and slow. The ideal solution was a new and closer river terminal. The plan that evolved identified a site directly west of Fort Leavenworth at the point where the Republican and Smoky Hill streams joined to form the Kansas River (map 1). From this location, soldiers could easily patrol large sections of both the Oregon and Santa Fe Trails, and freighters could more efficiently supply the forts farther west. Fundamental to the success of the scheme, of course, was the feasibility of navigating the 169-mile length of this stream westward from Kansas City. Major Edmund Ogden, one of the two men who selected the new site in 1852, wrote the next year that he believed such navigation was practicable during the high-water season from late spring into early summer. The encampment opened in 1853, and when steamers made six successful trips on the route in 1854, Ogden's belief seemed more than justified.[7]

It did not take people long to speculate that the same advantages that would make Fort Riley a good supply station could bring prosperity to a city located in its shadow. Talk was in the air almost immediately that a military road would soon connect the site with Fort Leavenworth. These factors, when combined with the imminent opening of Kansas Territory to public settlement in late 1854, made the prospects for a new town site here among the best in the country. Nearly everybody understood the possibilities for military contracts and the collective buying power of a military payroll. Bigger thinkers, though, envisioned metropolitan status for this place—a true gateway city. Because the site stood at the eastern boundary of the Great Plains and at the head of river navigation, it could become a trade emporium for the products of the eastern and western halves of the nation. A city here might easily surpass Kansas City in that commercial role, just as Fort Riley was about to replace Fort Leavenworth as a military supply base. Other schemers soon added the obvious possibility of making this site the capital of the new territory and future state.[8]

Officers at Fort Riley were in an excellent position to participate in any town-founding schemes. Several had just participated in a similar and highly successful enterprise that had established the city of Leavenworth. They urged the new post commander, Colonel William R. Montgomery, to withdraw from the military reserve a choice, 320-acre tract of riverfront

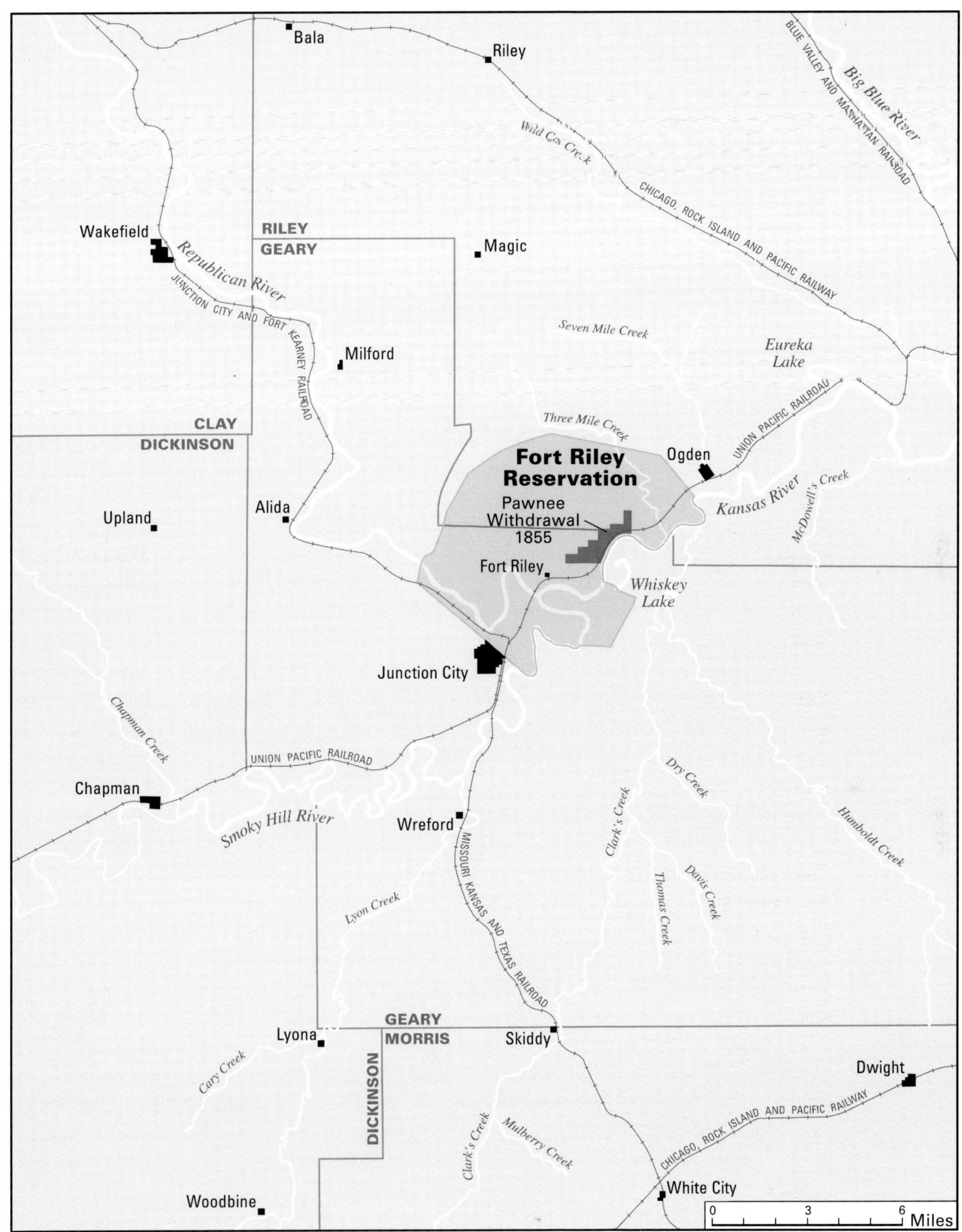

Map 1. Junction City and Vicinity, circa 1900

property for a site. He did so, and by September 1854, the Pawnee Association had been formed with twenty-five members. These included Montgomery himself as president and Andrew Reeder, the new territorial governor. Reeder agreed to convene the first session of the legislature at Pawnee the following July if a building were available. Post sutler Robert Wilson (another member of the association) therefore hurriedly oversaw the construction of a two-story stone structure. He finished on July 1, the day before the session met.

The Pawnee scheme had an excellent chance to succeed. Had it done so, it would have usurped all the roles that Junction City later assumed. The plan collapsed almost immediately, however, mostly a result of personal feuds. The proslavery majority in this legislature distrusted the Pennsylvania-born governor and objected to any location so far from the settled areas along the Missouri border. They voted for an adjournment two days into the session and then reconvened later that month at Shawnee Mission, near Kansas City. Next, enemies of Montgomery within the army brought charges against him for evicting a family that legally owned acreage within the Pawnee tract. Scandal-fearing officials in Washington reacted to these events by removing Reeder from office and transferring most of the remaining military members of the town company to other posts. Pawnee died quietly, almost before it had begun. A cholera epidemic at the fort in late July was the final blow. Officials restored the 320 acres to the Fort Riley reservation, and potential town founders had to seek other locations.[9]

Disappointed speculators left the Pawnee site reluctantly, but not the general area. Early in 1856, some moved directly across the Kansas River, where they laid out Riley City. Others platted the community of Ogden just beyond the reservation line on the east. Neither of these locations was ideal. Riley City, although close to the post, occupied a flood-prone and unhealthy lowland site. Ogden was better situated but suffered because more than six miles separated its buildings from those of the fort.

The future site of Junction City, adjacent to the military reservation on the southwest, was closer to the post buildings than was Ogden. It was a few miles upstream from the actual river junction but on a low platform of land above the floodplain. Nearby Smoky Hill offered several good mill sites. Given these advantages, one would have expected a frantic scramble for the property. Activity did occur, but strangely, no settlement took place for over two years after the collapse of the Pawnee Association. The cause of this unexpected and significant delay was contested land titles. A group called the Cincinnati and Kansas Land Company filed the initial claim quite early, in May 1855. It named the place Manhattan, purchased a steamboat, and recruited settlers to travel from Ohio. All went well until low water forced the boat aground just above the mouth of the Blue River, no more than twenty miles from their destination. While the stranded travelers were waiting for the water to rise, people living nearby invited them to join their settlement instead of pressing ahead. The Blue River settlers even agreed to change the name of their community from Boston to Manhattan in order to fulfill a requirement in the Ohio company's charter. The passengers found the offer too good to decline.[10]

The steamboat incident, though fortunate for life in the new Manhattan, produced chaos at the future site of Junction City. The captain of the steamer, Hiram Millard, decided to proceed upstream on his own. He rechristened the company's plat Millard City and wrote back to Cincinnati for additional financial assistance. No money was forthcoming from that source, however, so Millard abandoned the project, although perhaps not before taking several thousand dollars from the sale of lots.[11]

With the departure of Captain Millard, any new developer of this site now faced two problems. Did the Cincinnati company still hold title to the land? And if not, would the new developers be liable should people who had purchased lots from the former owners file lawsuits? This conundrum meant no activity at the river junction throughout 1856. In the summer of 1857, however, Robert Wilson (the sutler at Fort Riley who had been in the Pawnee group) and four other local men decided to assume the risk. They renamed the site Humboldt, but then stopped activity for some reason, having built no buildings and sold no lots. The delay proved to be only temporary. Two of the five entrepreneurs, Wilson and James R. McClure, soon joined with three new partners, and Junction City as we know it today was finally surveyed in the winter of 1857–1858. The Cincinnati people protested mildly in 1858 and then legally in 1859, but they never made their case. Neither Millard nor the claimants from his supposed sale of lots ever materialized.[12]

A delay in town founding from 1855 until late 1857 may seem trivial at first inspection, but it seriously undermined the original dreams that Junction City might become the leading commercial city of Kansas or be named its capital. Lower water levels in the Kansas River during the seasons of 1855 and 1856 damaged belief in the regular navigability of that stream, for one thing. More important was a tremendous increase of more than 50,000 people in Kansas Territory during those years. With this growth had come the formation of major power groups in other cities: Atchison, Lawrence, Leavenworth, and even Manhattan. These places would now be intense competitors for the acquisition of government institutions, transportation routes, and other agents of economic development.

The town fathers of Junction City decided to concentrate initially on gaining control over local affairs. They recognized Ogden as their most serious rival for the Fort Riley trade and set about to reduce its influence. Ogden in 1859 was a formidable place. Not only did it enjoy proximity to the fort, it also commanded prestige and power from having been named the county seat for Riley County in 1856 and becoming home to a U.S. Land Office in 1857. Both of these honors accrued to the town largely because of geographical considerations. The southern boundary of Riley County at that time followed two river channels: the Kansas westward to Fort Riley, and then the Smoky Hill to the Dickinson County line. This delineation placed both Manhattan and Junction City in the same county and meant that neither community occupied even close to a central location within that political unit. Ogden, with its midway position east and west, had been an easy compromise choice as the seat.

Junction City leaders decided that the solution to their trouble lay in cooperation with Manhattan. The two groups joined to lobby the territorial legislature for a change in the boundary. This move was tactically brilliant for Junction City, because Manhattan had the population size and its representatives had the free-state political credentials necessary to influence this body. By 1860, the land office had been moved to Junction City and a new county line drawn. The border now left the channel of the Kansas five miles below Ogden and cut due west through the military reservation until it hit the Republican River. The main post buildings and Junction City, all south of this line, now lay in Davis County. This move was ideal from a Junction City perspective. Although Davis was a relatively small political unit, it contained only the flood-prone Riley City as a potential political and economic rival. When a county-seat election was held in June 1860, Junction City won easily, even though census officials recorded only 217 residents in the young community.[13]

Efforts by Junction City people to move beyond their initial political success were frustrated by the realities of the Civil War. Fort Riley was soon reduced to a skeleton garrison of about a hundred men, and the entire westward expansion of settlers and money stopped almost completely. What good was having a new land office if nobody came? Where was the profit in having a steamboat landing if no one docked? The transformation of Kansas from territorial to state status in 1861 came in the midst of this despair. When the newly elected officials passed out their allotment of prison, college, and other institutional prizes, Davis County residents could muster neither the finances nor the population numbers to launch a serious bid. These awards all went either to the relatively populous eastern cities that had blossomed during the boom years of 1857–1859 or to traditional free-state centers such as Manhattan and Osawatomie.

Few records survive of the private thoughts of local entrepreneurs during the early 1860s. It seems inevitable, though, as the war began to wind down after 1864 and thoughts returned to how best to compete in the business of economic growth, that railroads would be an obsession. Nearly every observer realized by this time that traditional strategies about transportation had become outdated. Railroads would be the principal instrument of development in the West, not roads and rivers. During the war years, locomotives had proved themselves to be much more reliable than steamboats, and they obviously could range far beyond the nation's limited network of navigable streams. Also, by being able to gobble up miles at previously unimagined rates, railroads were creating a whole new theoretical geography for cities. A well-established community at a railroad node could now serve a much larger trade area than before. A complex new game of political and economic maneuvering was afoot.

Junction City, which still had a small population at this time, would seem to have been at a disadvantage in the posturing for railroads. It was fortunate, however, in its location and history. The only Kansas railroad that had achieved an adequate level of financing before the war, the Leavenworth, Pawnee and Western, was projected to come right by its doorstep. The *Pawnee* in the name referred to the old town site on Fort Riley. Even though the state capital had gone elsewhere, the north bank of the Kansas River through Fort Riley and Junction City remained the most logical path for any entrepreneur who wished to build west from Leavenworth or Kansas City.

During the war, the Leavenworth, Pawnee and Western received an additional economic boost when influential politicians from Saint Louis and elsewhere in Missouri and Kansas got it named as one branch of a new government-subsidized line that would span the continent for the first time. The Kansas enterprise, now bearing a more prestigious name—Union Pacific Railroad, Eastern Division—began construction in 1863. Although war-related and other problems slowed progress, no one doubted either the importance or the inevitability of the line. In anticipation of a boom, the population of Junction City rose from a few hundred in the early 1860s to 3,002 in 1865, and many additional former soldiers poured in once the armistice was signed. Tracklaying was completed over the Republican River and into town in November 1866, and the workers halted there for the winter. For the next few months, the town was a businessman's paradise. Homestead activity at the land office was brisk to say the least, and saloons sprang up overnight. The basic activity was trade. Goods came in by rail and were dispersed by incipient wholesalers and freighters. Shipments went throughout central Kansas, of course, but also far beyond to Santa Fe merchants, Colorado miners, and an array of isolated soldiers. Streeter and Strickler, a firm that operated from a building at the southeast corner of Seventh and Washington, dominated this enterprise, employing hundreds of men and shuttling all manner of cargoes. Among the more modest businesses were those begun in 1865 by Bertrand Rockwell and W. W. Sargent, who invested their war savings in a general-merchandise store and a drugstore, respectively. Both enterprises were to endure well into the next century.[14]

The delay in the construction of the Union Pacific at Junction City during the winter of 1866–1867 was not caused by cold weather. It was intended to give railroad owners in Saint Louis time to lay out a new route to the West. The federal legislation that had established the Pacific railroad plan required the Eastern Division to run track northwest from Junction City up the valley of the Republican River and into Nebraska. There, at the one-hundredth meridian, it would join with other branches to form a single line across the western plains. The Saint Louis owners, however, envisioned greater profits from their road if it became a competitor for the Nebraska route rather than a complement to it. Wanting a direct line west to tap the gold fields near Denver and the Utah settlements beyond, they so petitioned Congress.[15]

Before the legislators acted on a new railroad bill, they listened to arguments from both sides. Nebraskans, Chicagoans, and others who would profit from a single northern line were against the change, of course; so were the people of Davis County. With the original route, Junction City, at the place where the rails abruptly changed direction, would be able to maintain a significant overland freighting business to Colorado, Texas, and other destinations to the south and west. With the new alignment, however, the town might easily become nothing more than another station on the line.[16]

Because the people in Junction City could not match those in Saint Louis in political power, they could only watch with sadness as the first train moved west from their community in May 1867. Still, they now had sufficient numbers and wealth to plan at least modest schemes of their own. They worried primarily about the future of Fort Riley. With the Union Pacific moving farther across the plains, the quartermaster depot that supplied western forts would likely be transferred as well. That event, in turn, would almost surely mean the closing of Fort Riley. Current readers, looking back on this problem and knowing the future importance of this post, might expect to see a spirited local fight to save the reservation. Instead, residents took the more realistic stance that closure was inevitable. In fact, once the army announced that the supply depot was indeed going to be transferred to Fort Harker (near Ellsworth) in July 1867, local citizens began to lobby government officials to sell off the reservation land as fast as possible. Doing so would create room for new farmers and others who would trade in Junction City. As a part of this effort, a group of local businessmen concocted a successful plan to gain title to an especially valuable 4,000 acres of the reservation that lay south of the Republican River and immediately adjacent to the town. They offered to accept this land as payment for rebuilding the main bridge across the Republican. A deal was struck, with the title passing in 1868, and the men quickly platted much of it as an addition to the city north and east of Eleventh and Washington Streets. The owners even managed to retain the property after their shoddily constructed bridge collapsed nine years later.[17]

To overcome the anticipated loss of Fort Riley, the local consensus was to embrace the technology of railroads completely. If Junction City could no longer be important as a connector between water and trail or between railroad and trail, why not make it a junction of a third type, between two or more separate rail lines? One feeder track easily could be constructed up the fertile Republican Valley as the Union Pacific had planned. Another possibility, which had already been under consideration for several years, was to join forces with Emporia businessmen for construction of a line to the south. The Neosho River headed just south of Davis County, and its valley then broadened into the richest lowland in the state. A railroad south along it assuredly would be profitable. Moreover, with an extension into Texas, a port could be established on the Gulf of Mexico for the shipment of Kansas grain.[18]

Both of the railroads discussed in the critical years of the late 1860s came to pass. The first to build was the Neosho line, which began life as the Union Pacific, Southern Branch, but soon became known as the Missouri, Kansas and Texas (MKT or "Katy") road. This was a successful venture in many ways, from its initial tracklaying in 1868 to its amazingly fast completion to Texas in 1872 and a connection with the coast. A need for outside financial help quickly led to a loss of local control, however. Junction City men held two seats on the board of directors in 1868, but none in 1869. Four years later, these new owners moved the repair shops for the line from Junction City, where they had been located as part of the original company plans, to Denison, Texas. With them went several hundred jobs. The pain of losing the Katy shops was somewhat assuaged by construction of the Republican Valley railroad. This one, called the Junction City and Fort Kearney, began construction in 1872. And in return for the county's support in the form of $150,000 in bonds, the directors agreed to locate their shops in Junction City.[19]

The possibilities for economic growth in central Kansas came fast in the boom years that followed the Civil War. New counties were established almost faster than the mapmakers could record them, and the agricultural frontier pushed westward for several periods at the astonishing rate of 100 miles per year. New towns gave competition to older ones, and local leaders had to make quick decisions about how best to invest their energy. One of the first potential windfalls from having the new Union Pacific connection into Kansas City came in 1867, when an entrepreneur named Joseph G. McCoy proposed driving large herds of cattle from Texas to the railroad for shipment to eastern markets. In his memoirs, McCoy wrote that he favored Junction City as the shipping point but that a landowner there (said to be the firm of Streeter and Strickler) gave him "a flat refusal to sell at any price." This decision probably was the result of pressure exerted by local ranchers, who were afraid of a tick-borne cattle disease known as Texas fever. McCoy, as has been well documented, then turned to a small town in the next county and made Abilene into the region's first great "cow town." Still, he could not resist a good jab at his first choice: "So by that one act of donkey stupidity and avarice Junction City drove from her a trade which soon developed to many millions."[20]

Joseph McCoy probably shed no tears in 1870 when Streeter and Strickler went broke after the collapse of its freighting business. The new railroads that the town had helped finance certainly boosted the local economy, but in the face of new communities and rail lines farther and farther west, it was difficult to do more than hold even. The population of Junction City peaked at perhaps as high as 5,000 in about 1868, but then, as the Union Pacific pushed on toward Denver and the quartermaster depot left, it soon fell to a level that vacillated between 2,000 and 3,000. The business of county government remained. So did that of supplying trade goods for the surrounding farm country. Beyond these things, jobs were scarce. The small shops of the Junction City and Fort Kearney Railroad (which was never built farther than Belleville, Kansas, and became a branch of the Union Pacific) employed about a score of men. Cornelius Fogarty became another economic mainstay after 1874 when he completed a dam across the Smoky Hill just southeast of town and began to operate a large flour mill.[21]

The people of Junction City in the 1870s seemed poised to let go of their past dreams and to accept a more conventional existence as a typical county-seat community. Fort Riley still set the town apart, of course, but the life span of the post seemed nearly over. What many people in town did not realize was that the reservation continued to serve one important role for the army. It was the principal hay field for most of the U.S. Cavalry, the supplier of feed to posts all across the West. This activity was not noticed, perhaps, because it seemed so mundane. Hay is not normally an especially valuable product or one associated with long shipments. In this case, however, the practice made sense. Arid climates and small post sizes combined to make hay a scarce commodity on the High Plains. Fort Riley, in contrast, was far larger than most posts, and its 20,000 acres of Flint Hills soil produced superb native forage.[22] All that was needed was an efficient way to transport the crop, and the Union Pacific provided this in exemplary fashion (fig. 7).

Perhaps the biggest irony in the history of Junction City is that the network of railroads built to save the community in anticipation of the closing of Fort Riley turned out to be a principal reason why this post was spared and then enlarged and made permanent. The thinking began with army insiders. They noticed the ease of moving hay long distances from central Kansas and began to realize that this same practice could be applied to troops. Then, as the Indian wars began to ebb in the late 1870s and officers saw the need to consolidate garrisons, Fort Riley looked better and better. It had the acreage necessary to house and train a large force and the excellent rail connections required to dispatch men quickly to the location of any crisis.

Troops from Fort Riley demonstrated the practicality of this theory of centrality and mobility several times around 1880. They were dispatched to southern Kansas to help control "boomers" bent on settling within Indian Territory, to Saint Louis to maintain order during a railroad strike, and to the Ute and Navajo reservations for border disputes. Soon the general idea became the official recommendation of top leaders. Lieutenant General Philip Sheridan, for example, in reporting on the division he commanded, wrote to the secretary of war

7. Hay Camp, 1895 (print 13.12). The awarding of the hay contract for Fort Riley was major economic news in Junction City each year from the 1860s through the 1920s. Dustin Sands, a retired army colonel, won the job for 1895 with a bid of $12,600 to cut and deliver 2,400 tons of native grass from the reservation property. He and his large crew began August 1, finished in late September, and endured twelve rains and four bad winds. Having paid out $9,000 for labor and supplies, Sands made a substantial profit (*Junction City Union,* July 27, 1895; October 5, 1895). Note how the beds on the wagons have been expanded so as to haul the bulky hay more efficiently. Tents and a brush arbor, which loom over the heads of workers on the right, suggest the semipermanent nature of this enterprise.

in 1883 that "the extension of railroads in all directions over the vast region between the Missouri River and the Rocky Mountains now affords an opportunity for concentration . . . and economical results are anticipated."[23]

Because he was named commanding general of the entire army shortly after he wrote the preceding lines, General Sheridan was able to put his plan into motion. Fort Riley, he said, with its bluestem grass and varied terrain, would be an ideal place not only for a permanent garrison but also for a cavalry school. It took two years to lay the political groundwork for the concept of consolidation, but in 1885, Congress appropriated $30,000 for new barracks and officers' quarters at Fort Riley. Another allocation two years later, this time for $200,000, assured that the decision would be a long-term and large-scale commitment.[24]

It goes without saying that Junction City people were elated by all the activity at the fort. The expansion was a godsend and was truly appreciated after the earlier losses of railroad shops, the quartermaster depot, and more. Ironically, however, beyond voting for the railroad bonds some twenty years before, local entrepreneurs had little causal role in the post's revival. The only important exception was a letter-writing campaign in 1888 by George W. Martin and Bertrand Rockwell. Rockwell, a retired army captain who had become a merchant in town, learned from friends at Fort Riley that Preston Plumb, one of the U.S. senators from Kansas, thought that the fort mattered only to Junction City people, not to Kansans in general. Thus he was not pushing hard for new appropriations. The captain relayed this information to Martin, a former longtime editor of the *Junction City Union* and now a publisher in Kansas City. Martin, in turn, wrote an inspired editorial and got it reprinted in papers across the state, pushing Plumb and others in the state political delegation to renewed action.[25] As the new Fort Riley emerged, Sheridan became a cherished name in Junction City; Martin and Rockwell were only slightly less revered. Since the general never posed for Pennell, a portrait of George Martin seems an appropriate way to symbolize the initiation of the city's golden years (fig. 8).

A Tour of Washington Street

The federal appropriations for the renovation of Fort Riley, which totaled more than three-quarters of a million dollars between 1885 and 1891, set Junction City on the immediate course to the prosperity it exhibited when Joseph Pennell arrived on the scene. Indeed, Pennell, like most of the other businessmen in town, would never have come had the boom not occurred. Historian William Dobak has estimated that more than half of the construction dollars for the post during those years went to contractors from Davis (state legislators renamed it Geary in 1889 over local objections) and Riley Counties.[26] The total impact of such money was staggering. Although impossible to calculate or even to imagine completely, certainly some of the repercussions can be seen in the photographs that follow. They appear as extra touches of quality in the courthouse architecture and in the women's clothing. They are visible, too, in the range of goods offered for sale by local merchants and in the confident look on most of the faces. Almost overnight, Junction City was transformed into a flourishing community. Because of its neighbor's growth, the town also became more purely military in

8. George W. Martin, 1904 (print 1225). Martin (1841–1914), a native of Pennsylvania, came to Junction City in 1861 and founded the *Union* newspaper, which he edited for over twenty-five years. In this role, he became the principal spokesman for the town. Outsiders referred to him as a "whiskyite" because he defended the city policy of regulating the saloon industry through a system of fines rather than following the state's prohibition law to the letter and having to deal with unhappy soldiers and freelance bootleggers (*Topeka Commonwealth,* July 27, 1884). Martin served as town mayor, register of the land office, and state printer. He also was a founder and secretary of the Kansas State Historical Society.

tone than it had been at any time since the 1850s. Never again would anyone see the place as a sleepy county seat.

Any visitor to Junction City in the 1895–1922 period would have spent much of his or her time on Washington Street. Washington was (and is) the local name for what Americans refer to generally as Main Street. In this instance, the roadway is laid out north and south and extends from a bridge over the Republican River at the north end of town to another over the Smoky Hill a mile or so south of the city limits. With the tracks of both the Union Pacific and the MKT nearly paralleling it on the east, an important east-west street (Sixth) crossing it at a right angle, and the courthouse sitting prominently a half block to one side, the pattern is classically midwestern (map 2). Such a street, geographer Richard Francaviglia tells us, functioned as the "heart of a small town" during this period, "a visible manifestation of its business and political activity, its life in particular, and American life in general."[27]

Francaviglia's claim is grandiose, but it echoes most of the recollections that have been preserved from those years. Retailing activities centered on this street, certainly, but also much more. Government services were nearby. So were train depots, meeting halls, churches, and libraries. Washington Street focused all this varied activity, serving as its hub and basic reference point. It was the place to see and be seen, the spot to affirm one's identity as a member of the community on a daily basis.

Although aspects of "Main Street" activity extended along Washington from Fifth Street to Tenth Street and even beyond, the two blocks between Sixth and Eighth formed an easily identifiable core. Pennell took many shots of this location, partly because he could get nice perspectives from the upstairs windows of many buildings, but mostly because these blocks buzzed with activity. Almost any American who examines a sampling of these photographs will feel an identity with them (see figs. 9–17). Perhaps surprisingly, this will be true whether or not that person has ever been to Junction City, because of the considerable similarity between one Main Street and another. Such similarity should not be unexpected. These places are business locations, after all, and they look the way they do for pragmatic reasons. Their linear arrangements are certainly not the most aesthetic design imaginable but are an efficient way to serve shoppers. In the same way, the impression of an unbroken facade at the street level is a product of high land prices and of generations of shopkeepers realizing that customers liked their stores to be close to one another. Large plate-glass windows, a cheap and effective advertising device, create a third unifying element.

Architectural style provides additional unity for the buildings on Washington Street and in most other midwestern towns. The popularity of Greek Revival structures had waned in the United States by 1850 or so, leaving the towns that emerged in the latter half of the nineteenth century to develop a new look. This image varied to a degree. Neo-Gothic influences affected some churches, and a few traditionalists remained true to Greek columns, but Junction City and most other business districts became dominated by what is known as Romanesque or Italianate design. Romanesque buildings are heavy, solid affairs, often constructed of brick or stone. They appealed to store owners because these materials afforded a measure of fire protection and, even more so, because solidity was a marketable image. Other traits of this style affect primarily the upper stories of buildings: an ostensibly flat roof hidden behind a

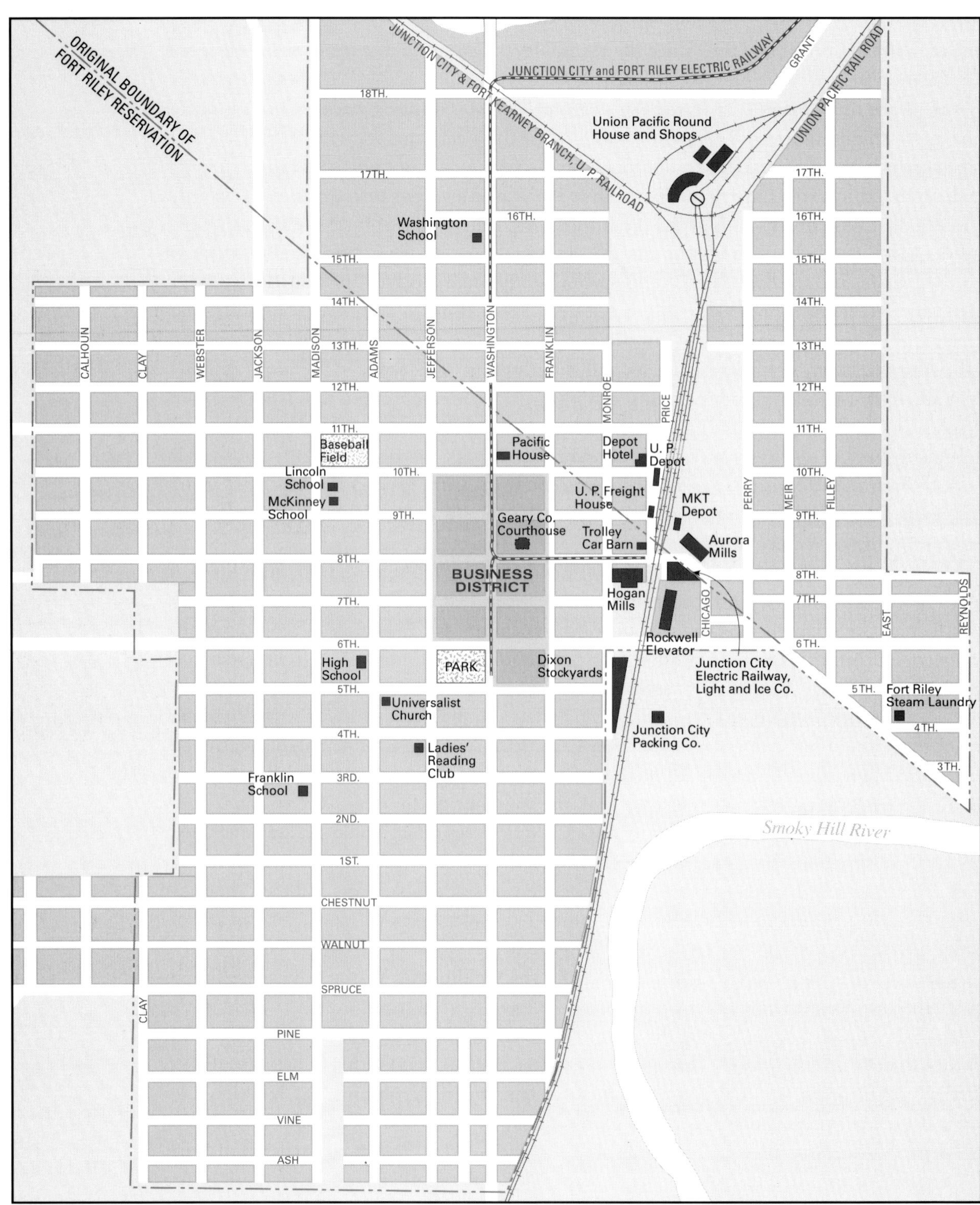

Map 2. Junction City Reference Map, 1900–1920

9. The 700-block (east side) of Washington Street, 1900 (print 568.1). Standing apart from the general array of horse-drawn vehicles on the street is a wagon entering the alley in the right foreground. Its thick wheels and low-slung bed are designed specifically to carry building stone. This photograph, although catalogued as part of the Pennell collection by Professor Robert Taft in the 1950s, is attributed to G. A. Streeter. The University of Kansas does not possess the original negative.

parapet wall, bracketed and heavily ornamented cornices, and windows in the shape of rounded arches.

A view of the east side of the 700-block provides a good introduction to North Washington Street (fig. 9). That this is one end of the business core is apparent from the abrupt change in building height and material. Something more than just Eighth Street separates the modest Farmer's Home Restaurant (with its name on the side) from the elaborate B. Rockwell Merchandise and Grain Company (the one topped with a flagpole). The Rockwell building is eleven years old in this photograph, having been rebuilt and enlarged after a fire. When a local newspaper editor called it "the pride of the city and the envy of our neighbors," the reference was both to the quality of goods inside and to the building itself.[28] The walls are constructed of local limestone, with bricks used as a facing on the front; these bricks, in turn, emphasize the heavy stone window arches. A triangular plate atop the cornice bears the date of construction (1889) and the family name.

The 700-block, like the others on North Washington, is broken midway by a service alley. Such alleys leave side walls exposed, and since these surfaces are both flat and highly visible, they usually became covered with advertisements. Here, the editor of the *Tribune,* one of four newspapers in town at the time, trumpets his identity and directs customers to a stairway that leads to a second-story office. These stairs and a series of smaller advertising signs are more clearly visible in figure 10, which peers down this alley in 1902. Just as at the corner of Eighth Street, it is easy to see that the decline in building height and quality away from the downtown core is abrupt. Note also the slab sidewalks leading across the dirt of the alley and to the foot of the stairwell. These were characteristic of Junction City at the time and, like the walls of the Rockwell building, were quarried from a local rock formation called Fort Riley or Junction City Limestone. According to Leo York, a longtime local mason, sidewalks were cut from a subtype known as yellow stone. This color was not popular for houses, but the layer was just the right width for a walking pavement. "It only had to be split one way and the top was nice and smooth." The York family and others installed over fifty miles of such walkways by 1901, an amazing total that was a boasting point for city leaders.[29]

The Romanesque look of the Rockwell building is repeated in another brick-faced stone structure immediately to the right of the alley. In between sit three more modest buildings: one with a Greek-temple motif on its second story, a modestly Romanesque design in the middle, and the rather neutral *Tribune* edifice. All three of these buildings house major retailers on their ground floors, but it is impossible to identify their names or products from the photograph. Part of the difficulty is the obstruction of awnings (they are unrolled because of the glare of the afternoon sun), but the bigger issue is that large signage was not necessary at

10 (opposite). Downtown alley, 1902 (print 855.2). Brand-name goods were making inroads on generic products at the turn of the century. Store owners vied to become "agents" or "headquarters" for these brands and then displayed the companies' advertising placards. The offerings here were for sale next door at the Hemenway Mercantile Company.

TRIBUNE
PRINTING
OFFICE
C.S. DAVIS
PUBLISHER
Best by Test
HEADQUARTERS
FOR
W.L.
DOUGLAS
SHOES
Agents
FOR
CHASE
AND
SANBORN'S
TEAS
AND
COFFEES

a time when carriage speed did not exceed ten miles per hour. The stores in question, by the way, are Brown's Harness Shop next to Rockwell's emporium and the large Hemenway Mercantile Company, which occupies two storefronts and is marked by a pair of matching awnings. Business seems to have been brisk on this October day.

The look and function of the east side of Washington Street continue if one moves a block to the south (fig. 11). This photograph was taken five years later than the one in figure 9, and the furled awnings tell us that it is a morning shot. The most obvious change is the addition of streetcar tracks down the middle of the street, although a close inspection also reveals that "Hall—The One Price Store" has been replaced by William C. Dumm's furniture company. Pennell made this exposure on September 12, while Junction City was hosting the annual tournament of the Kansas Firemen's Association. An estimated 400 men participated in the parade and then stayed on for a series of nine contests. Several of the competitions involved maneuvering large-wheeled, manual hose carts, two of which can be seen in the parade line. A "combination hook-and-ladder" race, which carried a prize of $50 plus the championship banner that is visible near the middle of the photograph, was won by the team from Clay Center.[30]

The mix of stores along this stretch of Washington Street was rich. Beginning at the alley in the 700-block and moving south into the foreground, one would pass Dumm's Furniture and Carpet, Loeb's Shoes, Starcke's Jewelry, Thompson's Smoke House, and then Miller's Drug Store on the corner. The 600-block begins with Pegues, Wright and Company (a department store). Next comes Loeb and Hollis's Popular Drug Store, a large "Zee-Dee" building still under construction, and Roesler's Market. The Zee-Dee label was derived from the names of its builders, Ziegler and Dalton, and the structure's obvious quality is a reflection of the success that J. C. (Charley) Ziegler, his brother Harrison (Hass), and their partner John T. Dalton had enjoyed over the previous decade and a half. They were major building contractors, first at Fort Riley and then at other posts across the country.[31] This edifice on Washington Street symbolizes the prosperity of the time as well as the close financial relationship that had come to exist between Fort Riley and the town.

The Zee-Dee was erected especially for Pegues, Wright and Company, an upscale establishment that was fairly new to Junction City and wanted to expand. The *Union* praised the design, especially its modern features. The first floor extended a full fifty feet in width, its reporter said, and had steam heat, toilet rooms, and "hundreds of electric lights." Leaded, "prismatic glass" over the transoms was (and still is) exquisite, but the most gushing words went to the pair of front windows: "They are the handsomest and largest . . . between Topeka and Denver."[32] The Zee-Dee's solid stone construction escaped mention, probably because that material was standard with Ziegler and Dalton. The newspaper also made no comment on how the Romanesque style of arched windows had given way to squarer and more subtle designs.

The tower of the Geary County Courthouse has long been a looming presence over the buildings on Washington Street. The details of this building, another product of the Ziegler and Dalton Construction Company, are discussed later. Its positioning in figures 9 and 11, however, nicely reveals the relative roles and strengths that people assigned to business and

11. The 600-block (east side) of Washington Street, 1905 (print 1636). Because the streets that intersect Washington are wider than alleys, advertisements on the sides of buildings there have increased visibility. George S. Spencer had a dental office upstairs from the Miller Drug Store. Two smaller signs reveal a similar location for Joseph Pennell's studio. Another sign worth noting—"Don't Spit on the Sidewalk"—is posted on the telephone pole nearest the camera. Spitting was a serious issue at a time when tobacco chewing was nearly universal among men. Long-skirted women objected and, for political leverage, joined their clothing concerns to issues of public health.

local government in Junction City and in many other plains communities in 1900. In the southern states and in older portions of the Midwest, the seat of the county government typically was honored with a central location, the familiar courthouse square. Businesses, less noble enterprises, clustered around it. This power relationship between government and business changed after the Civil War with the rise of American industrial and commercial strength. Courthouses in towns contemporary with Junction City, although still revered, were shunted to spaces not in high demand by retailers. Some went to a far end of Main Street; others, as here, to a site slightly off to one side.

Joseph Pennell photographed the firemen's parade from a window in Junction City's most famous building, a hotel called the Bartell House that had anchored the southern end of the business district since 1879 (fig. 12). The Bartell House had been constructed more as an act of faith than a solid business investment, for Junction City was not prosperous in the late 1870s. Its builders were two local men: Augustus H. Bartell, who owned a lumberyard, and John K. Wright, a contractor who had recently completed the grading work for the Junction City and Fort Kearney Railroad. They realized that the city would need a first-class hotel if it were to become a hub for business travelers and others brought to town by the new rail network, so they built it themselves. Bartell provided the materials, Wright most of the capital. At the grand opening in February 1880, they arranged for Governor John St. John, Colonel Pennypacker from Fort Riley, and the Sixteenth Infantry Band to greet an array of potential clients. They also solicited and received statewide newspaper coverage for their "commercial palace."[33]

Bartell and Wright decided that a mix of Romanesque detail and functional simplicity would best suit their business goals. They thus installed plain windows in most of the sixty rooms (later eighty-five), but arched ones at two focal points: the angled corner that faces the camera in figure 12, and over the canopy at the main entrance.[34] To hedge their financial bets, they also arranged for their "palace" to have storefronts on the ground level that could be leased for extra income. The town post office occupied the corner location for several decades. Also visible are the Shillito Music Store, the Holzschuher Drug Store, and Rudy Sohn's barbershop.

Figures 13 and 14 show the remainder of the Washington Street business core as it appeared around 1900. The bakery sign visible just beyond the alley from the Bartell House in figure 12 is on a building that, in 1899, had just become occupied by W. A. Bingham's clothing store. The Binghams moved to Junction City from Stockton, Kansas, after hearing praise about the town from a relative, Edward H. Hemenway, another merchant on Washington Street. The street itself dominates figure 13. Clearly it is not paved, but neither is it deeply rutted. This is a macadam, a fairly expensive but popular all-weather road of the time. To construct such a surface, one would begin with excavation and the placement of a bottom layer of coarse stone for drainage. Gravels of various sizes then would be added to create a slightly convex surface, and the entire mass would be compacted with a heavy roller. A macadamized street was solid, especially if gutters were included, as here. It was just as dusty as other roadways, however, and just as regularly strewn with manure. Limestone crosswalks helped keep shoes and hemlines clean.[35]

12. Bartell House, 1903 (print 947.1). A key to the success of any hotel in 1903 was good transportation service back and forth from the railroad depots. One of the distinctive carriages used for this purpose, known as a dray, is parked at the hotel entrance. It was owned by Marion H. Foss, who operated from a barn just west on Sixth Street.

13. The 600-block (west side) of Washington Street, 1899 (print 444). Seeing the running gear for ten wagons stretched along most of a block would inspire almost anybody to take a photograph. This string, a new shipment of "the famous Studebaker wagons," belonged to "Major" John Davidson, one of the many military veterans who had set up business in town. He owned a hardware store across from the Bartell House and was moving his wares from the Union Pacific freight house on East Eighth Street (*Junction City Union,* September 8, 1899). A hitching post is in the foreground.

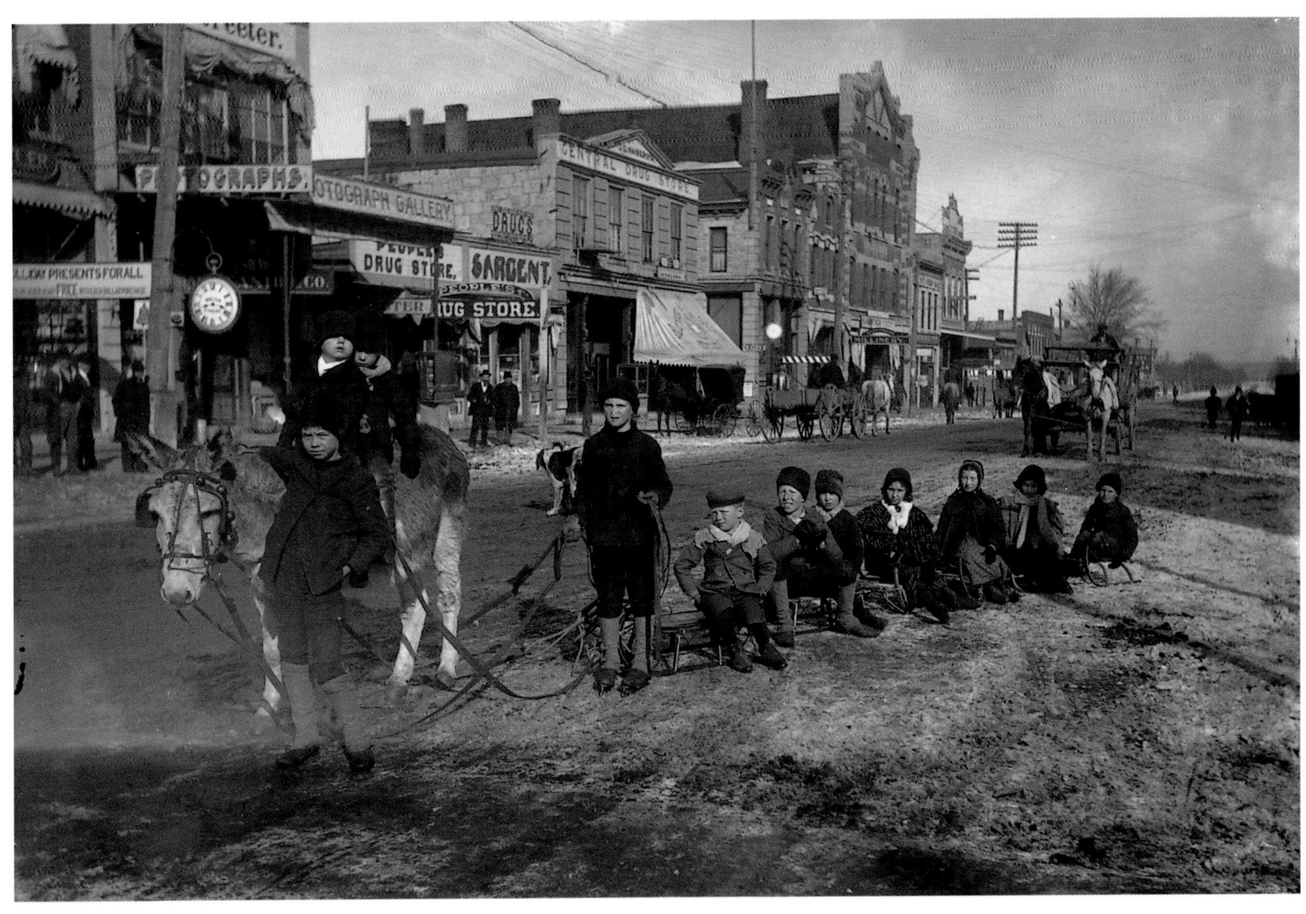

14. The 700-block (west side) of Washington Street, 1900 (print 523). Pennell labeled this photograph "Bessie Turner and Donkey Group." Although the line of sleds suggests that snow was imminent on this cold February 2, it had yet to fall. Harold Victor has identified the children from left to right as follows: Earl Parker, Clarence Victor, John Parker, Fred Shillito, Eugene Hall, Martin Hall, Dave Parker, Bessie Turner, Nina Watling, Grace Shillito, and himself (*Junction City Union,* April 29, 1955).

15. First National Bank, 1900 (print 545). A comparison of this photograph with figure 11 shows that Walter Starcke moved his jewelry store from one side of Washington Street to the other between 1900 and 1905. Note also the line of quality storefronts west along Seventh Street. This block rivaled the Washington Street core as a prime location for business.

North of the Bartell House, three buildings dominated the west side of Washington Street in 1900. One, occupied by the Waters hardware store, achieved dominance through sheer size, even though most of its three and a half stories was devoted to storage. The other two, the First National Bank at the corner of Seventh Street, and the Central National Bank, five buildings farther north, dominated in a more pragmatic sense. Lewis Atherton, the foremost student of social life in the late nineteenth century, has compared banks such as these to temples. They controlled money, of course, and money had come to symbolize the aims of an increasingly materialistic society. Bankers thus were expected to be priestlike—"conservative, closemouthed, wise, and dignified"—and the same was true for their buildings.[36] The owners of the First National (fig. 15) opted for a tasteful blend of the old (Romanesque details) with the new (two big plate-glass windows).

No portrait of Washington Street would be complete without a sense of its busyness. As in other towns of the period, all the stores opened early and rarely closed before nine at night. Saturdays, the traditional time for farm families to come to town, were especially hectic. The extremes, though, came when a popular merchant decided to advertise and hold a major sale. A good example took place August 1–10, 1901 (fig. 16). The merchant was Edward H. Hemenway, who operated a large general-merchandise store at 715–717 Washington and had begun to hold semiannual "nine-cent sales" in 1899. Each one was bigger than the one before.

A sampling of the Hemenway prices that hot August day includes ribbon at nine cents per yard, men's hats at ninety-nine cents, two pounds of peaches for nine cents, and kid gloves for seventy-nine cents. In addition, for the opening eighteen minutes of the day ("from nine minutes before 9:00 until nine minutes after 9:00"), one could purchase nine yards of the "best calico" for nine cents. The shadows in figure 16 suggest that Pennell was capturing this initial burst of activity. A reporter from the *Union* also was on hand. He wrote that "as the crowd surged in at the front door people were pushed out through the grocery department." Then, "as the ladies emerged, one could only imagine what had happened. . . . To the force of thirty clerks the eighteen minutes seemed like a day; but . . . everybody came out laughing, even if they did look as though they had been over the dam and had just come to the surface in the whirlpool below."[37]

Washington Street was anything but a static entity during the early years of the twentieth century. Beyond the temporary interruptions of sales, parades, and donkey sledders, store owners were jockeying for longer-term prizes. The more prosperous among them would move to larger quarters or annex the space next door. Others, perhaps underfinanced, would close soon after opening. A more enduring trend was the replacement of small wooden buildings with grander structures of brick or stone. The Bartell House, for example, had supplanted the older Hale House, which had burned in 1874.[38] Early within Pennell's period, Junction City merchants began to demonstrate their prosperity and faith in the future at an increased rate. Many of the handsome new stone buildings they erected on North Washington before 1906 still stand, including the Rialto at 605–607 (1897), the Caspar at 705–707 (1900), the Thompson at 703 (1905), and the Zee-Dee at 617–619 (1905).

Given the trend toward new construction, a plot of the wooden commercial buildings that remained downtown in 1905, some fifteen years after the business surge had begun, is inter-

16. Racket nine-cent sale, 1901 (print 717). The varied goods sold by Edward H. Hemenway (clothing, groceries, shoes, and notions) defined his business as a "racket" store. This label was common in the Midwest at the time. It probably refers to *racket* in the sense of a large and noisy party, the atmosphere prevalent (or at least hoped for) in such a commercial enterprise. Two baby carriages are in the right foreground. Long sleeves and hats are nearly universal attire, even though the date was August 1.

esting (map 3). The northeast corner of Sixth and Washington appears ripe for redevelopment, as does a pair of buildings on the west side of the 700-block. The choicest space, though, is where a series of small frame structures extends westward from the southwest corner of Seventh and Washington (fig. 17). Most of these units were rental property owned by a reclusive man named George Smith, who turned away all potential buyers. The ratio of wood to other building materials along Washington changes abruptly at Eighth Street. The construction of the Geary County Courthouse just east of this corner in 1899 was an indication that business leaders had wholesale renovation in mind for the 800-block, but as of 1905, a year-old stone building at 816 North Washington erected by Charles H. Baskin for his drugstore was the only progress visible.

A consideration of the internal geography of Junction City development also raises a bigger issue. Why was the heart of the town not platted originally farther north? Such a location would have reduced the distance to Fort Riley, to the mutual advantage of soldiers and merchants. It also would have been perfectly feasible in terms of topography. Washington Street has a gentle grade south of Sixth Street, where it ascends from the floodplain of the Smoky Hill, but north of Seventh Street, the route is nearly flat all the way to Eighteenth Street.

The town founders certainly wanted to be as close to the fort as possible. What restricted them was the boundary of the military reservation, a line that originally paralleled the Republican River about a mile to its south. This demarcation angled from northwest to southeast. It intersected Washington Street just north of Eleventh, the Union Pacific tracks near Eighth, and then extended on to a junction with the Smoky Hill (see map 2). A business district located between Tenth and Eleventh would have been possible in theory, but housing could expand from such a site only to the south and west. The angled border also meant that a depot site necessarily would be remote (somewhere south of Eighth), and that a bridge to the east over the Smoky Hill would be even farther south. After considering these realities, James McClure and others in the original town company decided that an initial focus on the 600-block was the proper compromise. Even though local entrepreneurs gained control of the reservation land south of the Republican in 1868, it was too late to change the basic pattern. The old borderline long paralleled the main road that led east from town to the bridge at Fogarty's Mill. It survives today in this vicinity as the modern city limits.

Inside the Stores

Although much can be learned about the values of townspeople from looking at streetscapes, it is human nature to want to venture under the awnings and into the shops. Pennell's photographs allow us to do this. His record is not complete, of course. For some reason, he took no interior views of the Rockwell store, the grandest one in town, or of the lobby of the equally elegant Bartell House. More understandably, the record for smaller, poorer businesses is meager. Most of his photographs were celebratory, taken soon after the store in question had either opened or remodeled. Since such events also were covered regularly by the local press, it often is possible to pair a contemporary description of the scene with a photograph. As a result, we are able to reconstruct not only a stroll down Washington Street circa 1905 but also a visit inside a fair sampling of the stores to see and hear what was on people's minds.

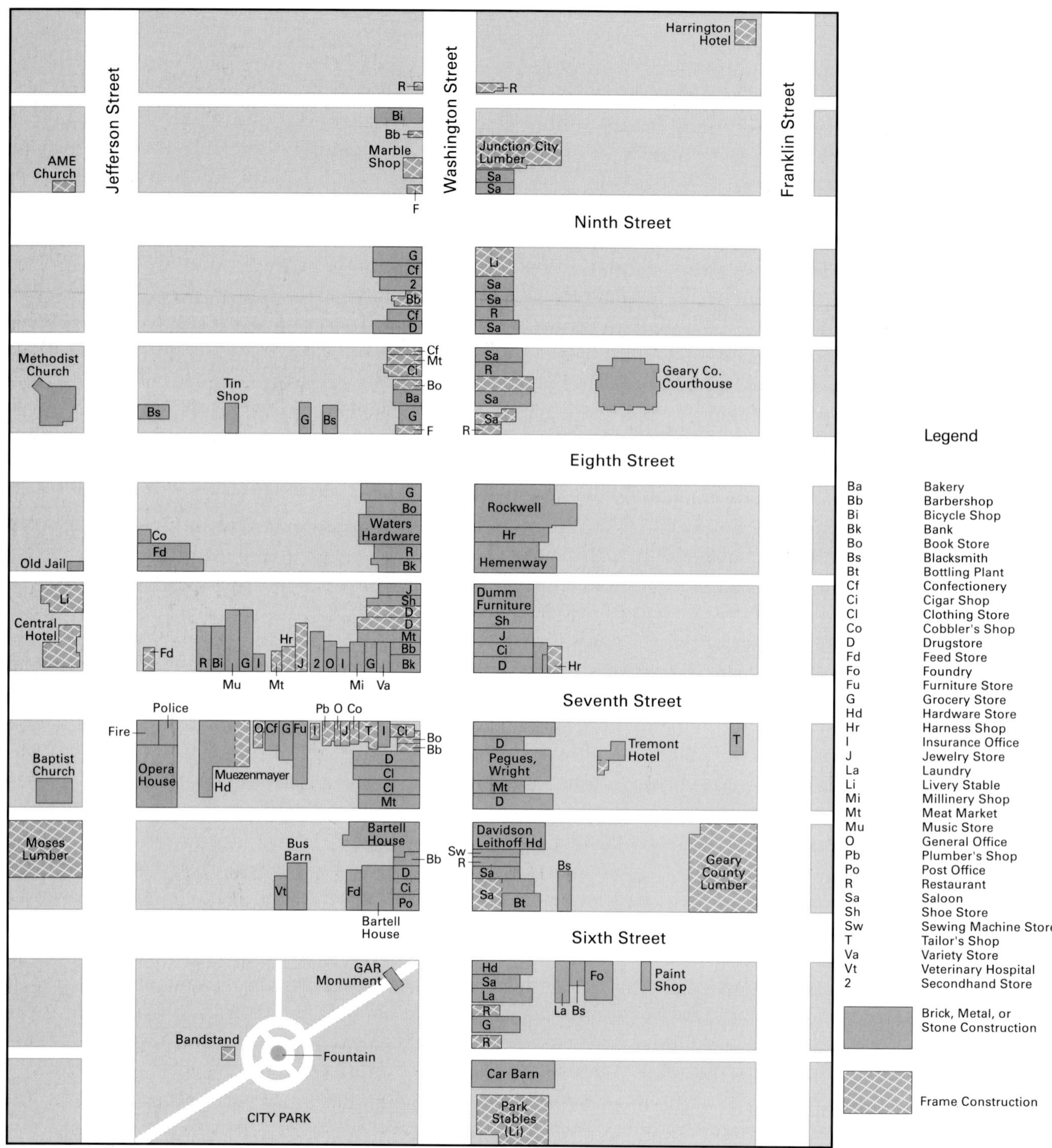

Map 3. Commercial and Civic Land Use, 1905

17. Corner of Seventh and Washington, 1906 (print 1652). Every town plan must provide office space for insurance salesmen and similar service people. Second stories on the main street typically housed most of this trade during Pennell's time, and outlying streets the rest. Junction City was unusual in having the offices of A. P. Trott Real Estate and J. S. Newman Merchant Tailoring located directly across from the First National Bank.

The retail scene early in the century was amazingly rich. A typical storefront was only twenty-five feet wide, which allowed as many as twelve different businesses on one side of a single block. It also was not difficult for a budding entrepreneur to get started. With stores so small, inventories could be purchased without much capital. Regulations were lax as well. Loren Reid, a Missourian who has written thoughtfully about these years, recalled the mood as informal:

> Any given store might sell unusual combinations of merchandise; a drugstore might stock drugs and toilet articles, but also might have wallpaper and even carpets. The owner of a hardware store might sell out and buy a grocery store, no doubt reasoning that if he could sell Moon buggies and Great Western Endless Apron Manure Spreaders he could sell anything.[39]

An inventory of the stores in Junction City at the time reflects the influence of Fort Riley, especially the unusually large number of laundries, restaurants, and saloons (table 1). Otherwise, the mix is typical. Three large general-merchandise businesses dominated the downtown district: Hemenway; Pegues, Wright; and Rockwell. Other oversized buildings were occupied by four hardware stores, which needed the extra room to accommodate their bulky wares. Elsewhere, small, fairly specialized stores were the norm. Eight doctors' offices were balanced by eight drugstores, six dentists by six confectionery shops. Butchers occupied separate quarters from grocery stores, and the importance of the horse was obvious from the presence of three harness shops and three livery stables. Bicycles were fashionable, but not yet automobiles. Another overview of Junction City retailing comes from one of the advertising signs popular at the time (fig. 18). The combination of feed, wood, and poultry at the Shaw Mercantile Company on West Seventh is evidence that unusual product mixes were not limited to Reid's community in Missouri.

Let us assume that our visit to downtown begins near its southern end on a weekday morning. Rudy Sohns's barbershop surely would be busy, because this was a ritualistic stop for many of the men who worked in this part of the business district (fig. 19). Sohns, along with John Fox, had been renting space in the Bartell House since 1897. His was a larger than normal shop, having three chairs, a shoe-shine stand, and, through the door, "complete bathroom fixtures, including two tubs and a water closet."[40] Barbershops were male worlds, of course, rich with raucous laughter and gossip about crops, sports, and the latest bidding for Fort Riley contracts. Some people would stop by just to visit, others to get a twenty-five-cent haircut. The baths were used primarily by travelers, since such conveniences did not exist in most hotels of the time.

Shaves were the heart of barbershop life. Two of the three customers in figure 19 are tilted back to enjoy this ceremony, an event that has been recalled fondly by almost everybody who experienced it. Lathering the face was followed by the gentle application of hot towels. The smell, the heat, and the reclining position all served to relax the customer while the barber stropped his razor and then expertly shaved and rinsed the prepared skin. An application of cologne and powder completed the rite, leaving the client "cleansed, refreshed, invigorated."[41] Reid has reported that a good barbershop shave would last for two, sometimes three days.[42] At the cost of ten cents, it was such a bargain that few townspeople shaved at home. They pre-

Table 1. Retail Stores and Service Establishments, 1905

Type of Goods	*No. of Stores*	*Type of Service*	*No. of Offices*
Bakery	3	Attorney	5
Bicycles	2	Bank	2
Books and magazines	4	Barber	7
Boots and shoes	2	Blacksmith	7
Cigars	3	Dentist	6
Clothing	2	Drayman	10
Confections	6	Hotel	5
Department store	3	Laundry	5
Drugs	8	Newspaper	4
Feed	4	Photographer	3
Furniture	2	Physician	8
Groceries	9	Plumber	2
Hardware	4	Real estate/insurance	10
Harness	3	Shoe repair	2
Jewelry	4	Stables	3
Lumber	4	Tailor	3
Meat	5		
Millinery	1		
Music	2		
Restaurant	10		
Saloon	13		
Secondhand	2		
Variety	1		

Source: George C. Peck, *1905 Directory of Junction City, Kansas* (n.p.: George C. Peck, 1905).

ferred instead to take regular breaks from their jobs to seek out the havens of Sohns and his colleagues.

Half a block south of the Bartell House and across the street from the city park was the Park Steam Laundry, the largest of five similar operations in Junction City (fig. 20). It was owned by Thomas Dixon, Jr., a man whose father had been an original settler in the region and who still ran a stockyard business from the small frame building next door. The laundry had been at this location since 1893, but the building was brand new at the time of this photograph. It was another product of the firm of Ziegler and Dalton, which erected it after a major fire the previous April. People admired the cut-stone front and its decorative "turret top."[43]

Laundries were patronized by a large portion of the Junction City population. Their equipment was far superior to anything available in the home, their service was good, and they spared individuals much heavy labor. Perhaps strange to us a hundred years removed

18. Advertising sign, 1900 (print 505). The size and exact purpose of this sign are unknown. It probably was created by William F. Durbon, co-owner of a painting and wallpaper business that occupied the floor beneath Pennell's studio until 1899. The Durbon name appears in the design's middle frame, part of a fanciful scene located far from Geary County. Signs similar to this were often used as curtains in local opera houses.

19. Rudy Sohns's barbershop, 1903 (print 981). Cabinets containing the privately owned shaving mugs of regular customers were the signature item of a traditional barbershop. Here they flank a door that leads to the shop's bathing tubs. The mugs were personalized in various ways—sometimes with initials, sometimes with symbols of the owner's occupation or lodge. The woodwork and other detailing in Sohns's establishment were more luxurious than most, probably because of his location in the prestigious Bartell House.

20. The 500-block (east side) of Washington Street, 1899 (print 475). The Park Steam Laundry, operating out of the new building in the center of the photograph, was not unusual in having its own delivery wagon. Grocers and other merchants did the same to offer efficient and personal service in a competitive environment. To the left of the laundry is the plain exterior of one of Junction City's dozen or so saloons. The Capitol, operated by John L. Upton, enjoyed considerable local status and catered primarily to lodgers at the nearby Bartell House.

from the scene, a laundry's business was confined largely to men's apparel. Historian Frederick DeArmond has attributed some of this distortion to a traditional male reluctance to do laundry. Beyond this, he wrote, women were "more reluctant to send their garments out—in part from having someone else handle their 'unmentionables' and in part from . . . [a] fastidiousness about their raiment." Also, women's clothes were "less standardized in cut and materials than men's, meaning that they are more expensive to clean for the customer and less profitable to clean for the laundry."[44]

The Park Steam Laundry was divided into three compartments: a cement-floored washing room at the rear, a large ironing room in the middle, and a combined sorting room and office at the front. The front was a male domain (fig. 21). Will Brazil, the person on the right, was in charge of the office. A different social structure existed in the ironing section. Although Charles Clark served as foreman, the bulk of the work in this hot and humid environment was performed by women (fig. 22). The photograph is dominated visually by a series of long belts and a drive shaft that brings power to three ironing machines from an electric motor housed in the back room. Such an arrangement inevitably produced squeaks and danger. The biggest belt powered a mangle, the latest technological innovation for ironing sheets and other large, flat items. Made in San Francisco, this particular version was over eight feet wide, carried 320 degrees of steam heat, and required four people to operate when at full capacity. It was said to be the largest in the state. Steam was wonderfully effective for reconditioning clothes (so much so that nearly all laundry owners inserted the word into their business names), but the heat sapped the strength and energy of workers. The woman in the center-right felt compelled to wear short sleeves—not an insignificant sacrifice, considering the standards for modesty at the time. Mostly hidden on the right side of the photograph are smaller ironing machines designed for detachable collars and cuffs.[45]

Customers had more choices for their grocery shopping than for any other type of business in town. The Hemenway and Rockwell stores both had large food departments, and at the other extreme, four or five small general stores were scattered throughout the residential areas. Midway along the continuum stood the three to four traditional grocers who operated downtown. G. A. Latham's store, located across the alley from the Bartell House at 616 North Washington, was one of the shortest-lived of this group (fig. 23). As might be expected, Latham promised "an altogether modern grocery and fruit establishment" when he opened in October 1901. The smile he showed for Pennell's camera on opening day did not last, however, and he returned to Boise, Idaho, after only two years.[46]

One of the reasons for Latham's short tenure in Junction City may be the prominent "No Credit" sign he hung at the back of the store. No merchant liked the bookkeeping and financial uncertainty associated with charge accounts, but the practice was an accepted part of retail life. According to common wisdom, only Sears Roebuck and other mail-order establishments could demand cash, because they alone had the volume sufficient to cut prices to an absolute minimum. Other than the sign, the Latham store is standard for the time. Clerks would take customers' orders either on the telephone or in person and then fill them personally. Self-service was a concept far in the future, largely because many of the goods were sold in bulk.

21. Receiving area of the Park Steam Laundry, 1898 (print 251.1). Shirts and collars are by far the dominant items in the hundred sorting boxes behind the table. Will Brazil, the manager, is busy wrapping a packet for delivery. The incandescent light fixture that dangles above his head was a rarity at the time, and the laundry boasted of having eleven of these new conveniences (*Junction City Union,* August 11, 1899).

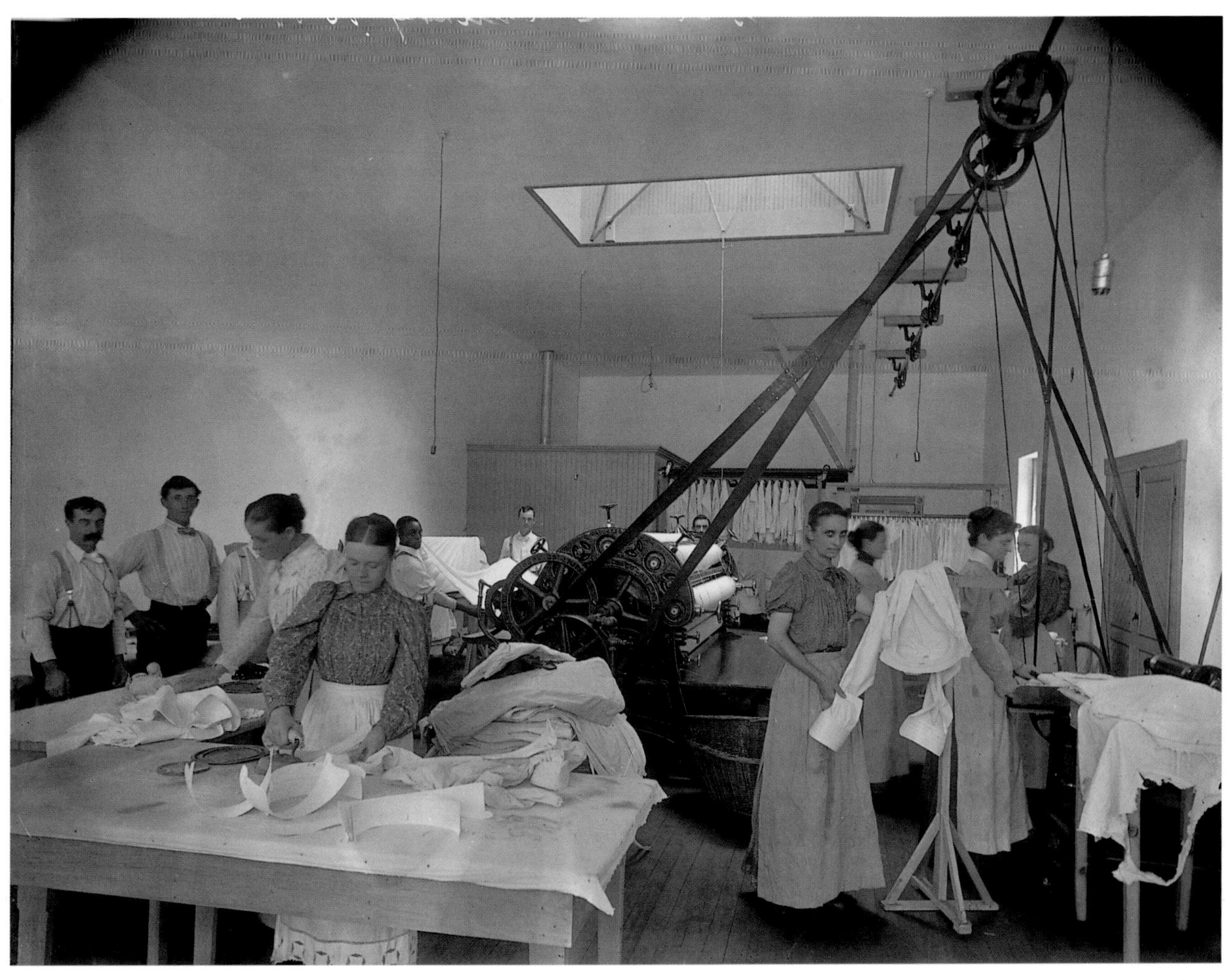

22. Ironing area of the Park Steam Laundry, 1899 (print 468.5). The group of women hard at work in this photograph contrasts vividly with the cluster of men watching from the side. One of the onlookers is Will Brazil, who also appears in figure 21. On the left, workers are ironing shirts by hand; at the center-right, another woman folds a shirt over a wooden frame. The partition at the rear sets off a "dry room," which was equipped with eleven racks each seven feet high (*Junction City Union,* August 11, 1899). The back door leads to a washing room.

23. Latham grocery, 1901 (print 797). A lack of refrigeration and questionable sanitation procedures created problems for grocers. They often felt obligated to buy what farmers brought in, even though they knew that many of the eggs might be fertile, some of the butter rancid, and some of the milk sour. Careful butter makers would counter this reality by marking their products in distinctive ways as a clue for discerning shoppers. Dairy products that stores could not sell often were shipped to regional creameries and then on to manufacturers. This process left a generation of rural people convinced that "store-bought" cookies and similar products contained highly suspect ingredients.

Having cookies and crackers stored in large boxes; beans, coffee, flour, and sugar in bins; cheese in wheels; and pickles and vinegar in barrels produced a blended aroma in grocery stores that was unforgettable. It also created multiple tasks for the clerks, who had to measure, dip, cut, and wrap efficiently while choosy customers looked closely over their shoulders. Latham's big-wheeled coffee mill is at the rear of the building, partly hidden by a stove. Rolls of wrapping paper and a spool of string are on the counter at the right rear, and bins for the various bulk goods line the wall on the left. On the near counter sits a set of balance scales used in the sale of bulk items. The mastery of these scales was perhaps the trickiest job for a clerk. As Frank Glick remembered from his years working in his father's grocery at 826 North Washington, the procedure was

> uncomplicated when it involved only weighing up an even pound, or two, or three, and multiplying by the price per pound. But it was a different matter when a customer asked for a quarter's worth of beans at fifteen cents per pound, or for a chunk of cheese which weighed one pound, seven and one-half ounces, priced at twenty-five cents per pound. The clerk had to do his own computing with pencil and paper—often on the same paper in which the cheese was wrapped. Weighing was the crucial act which tested the care and honesty, not to mention the arithmetic, of the store. Fred and Margaret [Frank's parents] were known to be very meticulous about it. It was remarked, with a smile, among their country friends that when weighing out a pound of crackers Fred would break the last cracker in two to get the weight exactly right, whereas Margaret would take out the whole cracker.[47]

A grocer dealt not only with bulk products. Canned goods were common, too, most of which carried brand names. A close look at the left side of the photograph shows the Club House label on many shelves and Richardson's Lemon Wafers on the wooden box. Butter, milk, eggs, and seasonal fruits and vegetables came from local farmers. Customers would ask especially for the products brought in by certain people.[48]

Across from Latham's stood John Davidson's hardware store. Davidson was a pillar of the community, having served on both the school board and the city council. He had been in the hardware business since 1885 and had moved into this particular two-story, 46- by 120-foot building (a former livery stable) ten years later.[49] Stoves were one of his standard items, and he offered a good selection (fig. 24). The ones photographed are cooking models, with the more basic designs in the front row. The oven is centrally located and lined with asbestos. To one side is the firebox (marked by an accompanying ash shelf), which could be equipped with a grate for either coal or wood. Many ranges have a porcelain-lined reservoir for hot water on the opposite side. It made sense to install such reservoirs on cooking stoves rather than on heating ones, since hot water and hot food were near necessities in both summer and winter. Bread boxes sit atop "high closets" (warming compartments) on the ranges in the rear. Nickel plating adds a touch of beauty.

Although newspaper editors and other community boosters certainly were proud of their barbershops, grocery stores, and hardware dealers, such enterprises never claimed the hyperbole given to the Bartell House, the Rockwell store, and our next stop, the Pegues, Wright Dry Goods Company. These last three were elite businesses, dealers in high-quality goods and services of the type associated with cities, not country towns. They represented a hoped-for future, a time when such stores would become more numerous and Junction City might truly rival Topeka and Wichita.

Lindsay Pegues came to town in 1900 along with two business partners. The *Union* noted that he had worked for eighteen years with the famous Crosby department store in Topeka and was now ready to open a similar business locally. Crosby's was a high standard, but the new establishment surpassed the editor's highest hopes—"twice as good as expected." Although stocked with a wide range of goods, the interior "present[ed] an appearance that catches the feminine eye. It is, in fact, a ladies' store, with everything from the ready-made suits to the lesser articles that go to 'round out' a fashionably dressed lady."[50]

Pegues prospered in Junction City. He doubled his floor space in 1905 with a move into the new Zee-Dee building at 617–619 North Washington, which had been designed expressly for the store's needs. At the grand opening, which featured the Ninth Cavalry Band from Fort Riley, the newspapers again gushed. In capturing the mood, Pennell worked hard to encompass all fifty feet of the store's width, an expansiveness that everyone noted with pleasure (fig. 25). Quality oak cases against the walls held dress goods and materials, while more centrally located glass showcases displayed embroideries, laces, and other notions. The store maintained separate departments on the main floor for suits, hats, dress goods, and even ribbons. A basement level stocked tinware, stationery, soaps, and china; a balcony contained a well-apportioned rest room.[51]

The millinery department at the new Pegues, Wright store was located in back of the dry goods, just out of camera view in figure 25. Pennell had ventured into this ultrafeminine domain at least once in the original store, however (fig. 26). Hats were far more important to people in 1900 than they are today. For both men and women, they were an essential part of being dressed. A range of choice existed for each sex as well, but this range was larger by far for the ladies. A good milliner's shop was part craft studio and part salesroom. Many of the hats in view had been purchased in completed form from wholesale houses, but others had been assembled by local designers using wire frames, straw shells, and a wide array of ostrich feathers, muslin roses, and imported silk ribbons. The terminology overwhelmed any male who happened near: sailor styles, mushroom brims, hussar turbans, and Gainsborough effects. Colors, too, were difficult to describe. Those for the 1909 season were said to be "mulberry, serpent and olive green shades, catawba, dull rose, and wisteria."[52]

The next stop on this hypothetical walk north along Washington—John Gartner's cigar store—is just across the street from Pegues, Wright, but about as far away from the millinery world as one could get. Society had labeled tobacco use by women to be immoral at this time, yet sanctioned its nearly universal consumption among men. Of Junction City's three tobacco shops, Gartner's at the corner of Seventh Street was the newest. As a first venture into retailing, he had bought out John Barth the previous May and had invested in expensive new display furniture (fig. 27).[53]

A careful examination of the shelves on the back wall reveals a few packets of cigarette papers, but this form of smoking did not become popular until after World War I. In 1900, most men regarded cigarettes as what their name literally implies: a small and definitely

24. Stove room in Davidson's hardware store, 1898 (print 269.4). Buck's, the company featured by Davidson's, is still in business today. A single model from a cheaper line, Peninsular, also is on display. Each of the four hardware stores competing in Junction City stocked a different brand of stoves. The same was true for the two other staples advertised on the wall posters: the Rook plow and Studebaker carriages and wagons. The girls standing on the platform at the right are entrants in an annual baking contest sponsored by the store.

25. Pegues, Wright and Company, 1906 (print 1777). The yard-goods department dominates the left side of the photograph, while shirtwaists, suits, and other tailored items occupy the right. Accessories in the middle include bead purses (fifty-nine cents), bracelets (thirty-five cents), collars, combs (twenty-five cents), and perfumes. Note the modern steam radiators hidden under the tables and a system of overhead baskets designed to convey goods and cash to wrappers and cashiers on the balcony.

26. Millinery department at Pegues, Wright and Company, 1903 (print 964). Although design variations in women's hats were nearly infinite, head size was of no concern. These hats perched atop masses of hair, not on heads directly, and were held in place by long pins. Wall hangings of sheer fabrics, ribbons at the ceiling, and suspended parasols create a festive atmosphere in this second-story room. The decorative draping at the rear is known as a rope portiere.

27. John Gartner's cigar store, 1900 (print 595.3). Gartner was nearly as proud of the new "inlaid linoleum" on his floor as he was of the oak cabinetry. Linoleum was a recently developed product, impressive in its range of colors and durability. This particular design imitated the look of tile. A spittoon on the floor suggests not only the prevalence of tobacco chewing but also the practicality of a linoleum floor as far as cleaning was concerned. Three incandescent bulbs are another indication of modernity. The knob-and-tube wiring visible on the ceiling is actually safer than later systems, because wires kept this far apart cannot possibly cause a short circuit.

effeminate version of the manly cigar. Gartner (the man in the hat) and his fellow shopkeepers actually manufactured several brands of their own cigars In addition to carrying standard national varieties. These are displayed in the double-deck case nearest the photographer. The Gartner name appears on boxes of Injunctions, a quality five-cent product "of the latest style" that he intended to be the "leader for the house." Coronada and General Sheridan, other nickel varieties, also can be seen, together with Red Snapper, Havana Rose, and Las Delicias.[54]

Two other products vied with cigars for space in the Gartner store. The back wall is stocked with bags of smoking tobacco, used mostly for pipes. The famous Bull Durham brand undoubtedly is there, but the only label clearly visible is Gold Band, marked at thirty and forty cents. Behind the cigar counter is a large stock of plug, or chewing, tobacco. This item was not as prestigious as cigars but was cheaper and more widely used. Whereas cigars required leisure and free hands to enjoy, one could chew while doing most any outdoor work. Chewing tobacco came in foot-long slabs that were notched to indicate pocket-sized plugs. A specially designed cutter (one is on the counter) would slice off the length desired.

Catercorner across the Seventh Street intersection from Gartner's stood another popular local establishment, the Corner Pharmacy. Profits in a traditional store of this type came primarily from the sale of prescription drugs, but success with the general public derived much more from the ice cream, carbonated treats, and friendly chatter dispersed in about equal amounts at its soda fountain. In 1899, store owners Albert N. Miller and Burt Shoemaker had just installed Junction City's newest and most elaborate version of these gleaming marvels (fig. 28). Manufactured by the John Mathews Company, their fountain featured sixteen syrup cans, a canopy of polished cherry wood that towered over ten feet above the floor, and a counter of genuine Mexican onyx.[55]

The connection between drugstores and soda fountains goes back to the early days of mineral spas. If mineral waters were an aid to health, it made sense to market them in pharmacies. After this it was only a small step to add flavorings to the waters and then for people to see them as a source of drinking pleasure. Coca-Cola, Pepsi-Cola, and Dr. Pepper all were invented by pharmacists; the mixtures were even championed by the Women's Christian Temperance Union as an alternative to liquor. Still, the transition away from medicine was incomplete in 1899. The owners of a local "pop" factory placed special emphasis on "the nerve tonic and indigestion cure features" of their products, and newspapers regularly carried ads that linked ginger and sarsaparilla—two of the products on this fountain's menu—with, respectively, indigestion and purification of the blood.[56]

Leo Loeb's shoe store stood three doors north of the pharmacy. This business, like most in Junction City, was highly competitive. The Hemenway and Rockwell stores both maintained large shoe departments, and John C. Teitzel, at 712 North Washington, had been a fixture in town since the 1880s. Teitzel not only sold commercial boots and shoes but also manufactured them. Officers at Fort Riley had been so impressed with his products over the years that he regularly received orders for military boots from all over the country; he even held a contract to outfit the graduating class at West Point.[57] Such was the business situation faced by young Leo Loeb as Pennell photographed him at 707 North Washington just after his opening

Menu
DONT CARE
COFFEE
NECTAR
ORANGE
BANANA
GINGER
WILD CHERRY
SARSAPARIL...
Menu
CHOCOLATE
PINEAPPLE
RASPBERRY
STRAWBERRY
LEMON
VANILLA
ROOT BEER
COCA-COLA

(fig. 29). Loeb (the man on the left) had followed his pharmacist brother Louis to town from Nebraska. He had learned the shoe trade at Grand Island and personally traveled to "the East" to purchase stock and fixtures. The store endured for only a few years, however.[58]

For a luncheon break after a morning tour of the stores, the place of choice for most middle-class Junction City residents would have been Mike Frey's Washington Restaurant in the middle of the 800-block (fig. 30). Eating out was not nearly the common practice in 1900 that it is now, and any town of this size that lacked a college or a military base would have supported far fewer than the ten restaurants shown in table 1. The Fort Riley connection also helps to explain Frey's location a block of so north of the main shopping district.

Mike Frey was a longtime restaurateur when he opened his new enterprise in 1908, having first bought out the Jenkins Restaurant with his brother Will in 1895. Will was the baker in the family, and Mike served as the convivial "front-end" man. By 1908, he had saved enough money to hire an out-of-town specialist for interior decoration, the firm of Parr Brothers, Vancil and Hearick. The *Union* reporter particularly admired the fashionable "mission style" furniture and the "French plate mirrors and shelves" that hung along the walls.[59]

Although Junction City's principal retail stores inevitably dominated the attention of shoppers, newspaper reporters, and photographers alike, these were far from the only important business activities in town. Many of the other, relatively hidden activities dealt in personal services and operated from small offices that did not require a traditional Washington Street storefront. Others in this group sold regular wares but kept away from the downtown core because of the location of their clientele (for example, a neighborhood grocery), their lack of money to pay the relatively high rents there, or perhaps their race or social standing. Still others dealt in products that demanded unusually large lots (such as lumberyards) or that generated odor or noise (such as livery stables and foundries).

All the doctors and dentists in town kept offices in the second stories of downtown businesses. So did most attorneys, insurance agents, and newspaper editors. In city directories, these locations are designated with standard street numbers, but in practice, people knew them as did O. R. Wibking, who gave the location of his dental office as simply "over Keller's" (see fig. 18). Narrow, dark stairwells wedged between storefronts provided access to these various quarters, but the rooms themselves usually were well lit. Pennell captured a typical example with the office of attorney J. B. Rairden (fig. 31).

Combinations of poverty and prejudice that could keep entrepreneurs from prime retail settings are represented by photographs of an unknown popcorn vender, shoe repairman James A. Counts, and the Hammond family laundry (figs. 32–34). Pennell observed the

28 (opposite). Miller and Shoemaker's soda fountain, 1899 (print 468.10). Burt Shoemaker was a part owner of this store only from 1899 to 1901. For most of its long life, it was simply the Miller Drug Company. The name Coca-Cola appears in special lettering on the fountain's menu, a reminder that it is the only brand name sold. A Junction City entrepreneur probably was the first person in Kansas to sell Coke. Druggist Linden S. Sargent heard about the product from a Fort Riley officer and began to put in regular orders to Atlanta (*Junction City Union,* April 29, 1955). Note the stack of glass holders on the back bar and their use by the two customers.

29. Leo Loeb's shoe store, 1904 (print 1277). Stocking a shoe store was a straightforward and relatively inexpensive process, which made this a good business for a young entrepreneur. Having the boxes in plain view is logical, but the long rows make an already narrow room appear even narrower. Most of the stores from this period, lined with shelves and poorly lit, were invariably somewhat gloomy. Loeb had invested in the latest multiple-bulb ceiling fixtures, but they were probably not enough to keep his fan palms healthy.

30. Mike Frey's restaurant, 1908 (print 2030). Along with buying expensive decorator furniture for his new store, Frey added many other elegant touches: a suspended birdcage, a Boston fern and fan palm near the entry, carnations and carefully pressed cloths on each table. His waitresses are immaculately clad as well, although perhaps a little nervous about the noon rush, since the clock reads 11:38. A telephone hangs on the wall above the fern. At the extreme right is a glimpse of the less formal counter section of the business.

31. J. B. Rairden's law office, 1900 (print 520). Rairden, an Iowa native, was admitted to the Kansas bar in 1890 and set up practice in Junction City seven years later. An interest in Republican state politics led him to move on to a larger city sometime before 1905 (*Junction City Union,* October 28, 1898; November 24, 1899). The books on his desk are the *Encyclopedia of Law.* A sign on the wall warns against spitting tobacco juice.

32. Popcorn man, 1904 (print 1370). The peanuts and fruit visible inside the stand have attracted a small crowd of jump-ropers. Pennell's advertising sign reveals that studio portraits, not landscape photographs, were his principal business.

33. Counts's shoe-repair shop, 1915 (print 2807). A newspaper article in 1918 reported that Counts employed six people and had purchased machinery worth several thousand dollars (*Topeka Plaindealer,* January 18, 1918). He also made it a point to teach his trade to young boys, five of whom are shown. Buffing machines are at the extreme right edge of the photograph; the wrapping paper found in every store is at the left.

popcorn stand daily, since it stood directly beneath his studio at the corner of Seventh and Washington. Most towns had at least one business of this type, often run by a physically handicapped person. Junction City hosted at least two. George Puffenberger, "a little crippled man," ran a tiny restaurant at 914 North Washington from before 1905 until just before 1920.[60]

James Counts was perhaps the first African American in Junction City to run a business that catered successfully to a general audience. A native of South Carolina, he came to Kansas while serving in the Tenth Cavalry. In 1914 he rented one of the small frame buildings on West Seventh, west of Gartner's cigar store, and opened a shoe-repair shop. No records exist about Counts's early finances or the attitudes of white citizens toward him. People of both races certainly must have talked, however, because the only occupations listed for black men in the city directory as recently as 1909 were as porters, in menial labor, or within the African American community itself (table 2). Counts's shop attained credibility once he had garnered

Table 2. Occupations of African American Heads of Households, 1908–1909

Men's Work	*No. Employed*	*Women's Work*	*No. Employed*
Barber	1	Cook	1
Clerk	1	Domestic	4
Cook	5	None listed	37
Fire stoker	1		
Hotel proprietor (National Hotel)	1		
Ironer	1		
Janitor	1		
Laborer	14		
Lamplighter	1		
Painter	1		
Pastor	2		
Plasterer	1		
Porter	20		
Restaurateur (National Hotel)	1		
Soldier	1		
Stonemason	1		
Teamster	3		
Waiter	2		
None listed	51		

Source: Prewitt Directory Company, comp., *Junction City, Kansas, City Directory for 1908–1909* (Springfield, Mo.: Prewitt Directory Company, 1909).

34. Hammond's laundry, 1903 (print 1030). The bicycle, a woman's model, suggests that a desire for exercise or practical transportation may have factored into the clothing selections of these women, not simply finances or social class alone. Note also the pair of oars that leans against the wall. The Hammond laundry was located only two blocks from the Smoky Hill River.

repair contracts from Fort Riley and other posts. Within a year, he moved the business into a substantial stone structure across the street at 118 West Seventh.[61]

Of the five steam laundries in Junction City in 1903, two were located on Fourteenth Street to be close to the big trade from Fort Riley, and two (including the Park operation) were downtown. This left no clear clientele for the fifth business, the one owned by the Louis G. Hammond family. The Hammonds called their operation the Fort Riley Steam Laundry, but with a location at the extreme southeastern edge of town, they were badly positioned for the military market (see map 2). The photograph we have reveals nothing about laundry facilities but a great deal about the dress of poorer townspeople (see fig. 34).

Fashionable women in 1903, and even those who toiled in the ironing room of the Park laundry (see fig. 22), would have selected clothes that defined their waistlines much more than did the dresses worn by the Hammond workers. No corsets are apparent in this photograph, and the woman with hand on hip next to the door is committing an even greater social sin by wearing in public a loose-fitting "Mother Hubbard" dress with no waist at all. In fact, the whole concept of a dress was out of style in 1903, having been replaced by the combination of skirts and shirtwaists (compare fig. 16, 25, 26, 28, and 30). Men's fashion, never as variable as women's, nevertheless shows several contrasts between social classes as well. Whereas workers downtown all wore white shirts with detachable, highly starched collars, two of those at Hammond's have donned more relaxed dark-print shirts with attached collars. The third man wears bib overalls, a concept first popularized in the 1890s.[62]

Although the Hammond laundry, several general stores, and a few other enterprises were scattered throughout the residential area, Junction City possessed only one secondary business concentration. This was a block of East Tenth Street, directly across from the Union Pacific Depot (see map 2). For reasons that were unclear to city officials at the time, this general area had never been well maintained. Despite serving as the main entrance to the city for all business travelers and as the point of departure for every local person on his or her way to Topeka or Abilene, it somehow remained "one of the disgraceful sights . . . on the Union Pacific between Kansas City and Denver."[63]

Pennell photographed the depot in 1915 (fig. 35). His purpose was not so much to display that serviceable stone structure as it was to highlight the completion of a landscaping improvement project nearby. This work, a small park near the building and adjacent Price Street, had been a cooperative endeavor between the city and the railroad. It included new ornamental trees, a drinking fountain, a light, and an impressive series of raised, 200-pound cement letters that spelled out the town name.[64]

The landscaping installed in that burst of civic enthusiasm in 1915 was successful in its way, but it did little to change the overall character of the neighborhood. Just across the street from the depot stood, logically enough, the Depot Hotel (fig. 36). With a fashionable mansard roof and large porch, it was not an ugly building, but a shadowy reputation is suggested by its lack of coverage in the local newspapers. Pennell labeled his photograph "Bowery Row," a direct reference to a saloon by that name just east of the hotel on Tenth Street, but also an allusion to a district in old New York City that was known for its cheap resorts and tawdry display.

35. Union Pacific Depot, 1915 (print 2809). The men looking up at the camera are city and railroad officials who have gathered to celebrate a joint landscaping effort and the installation of a new welcoming sign. More interesting is the view beyond the depot, an area Pennell called the Bowery district. The frame building on the left advertises very cheap accommodations ("Rooms 25 Cents"). Across the street are signs that read "cafe" and "lunch."

36. The Depot Hotel, 1903 (print 944). Pennell took this photograph while standing at the Union Pacific Depot. The house on the left and the turreted stone building framed by the two utility poles also appear in figure 35. The Overland Restaurant and two saloons—the Bowery and the Fontella—operated in the buildings just beyond the hotel. Perhaps because of the noise associated with saloons and railroads, the residential housing density was low.

The Depot Hotel undoubtedly served its share of legitimate travelers, but to Junction City residents, it was the focus of a district where soldiers came to drink and prostitutes to ply their trade. Although not the only site in town where such services could be obtained, it was the cheapest, the largest, and therefore the most notorious. Three incidents provide a sense of the atmosphere. In March 1895, Dr. Lamoile R. King had his rig stolen and wrecked. The culprit turned out to be a soldier known as the Montana Wonder who had imbibed "a dose of corrosive sublimate" at "the Kansas House north of the Depot Hotel." Another time, "Miss Mary St. Clair, a young lady of Bowery prominence . . . stood off one of the city officers with a knife and a gun, but she was 'gathered in' just the same." Finally, and more tragically, the shooting of two soldiers "in a house of ill-fame on East Tenth Street" in 1904 caused the commander at Fort Riley to restrict all enlisted men to the post for several weeks.[65]

The associations among saloons, prostitutes, and young soldiers are as old as recorded history. Given the presence of Fort Riley, therefore, one could have predicted the existence of a Bowery Row somewhere in Junction City. It also should come as no surprise that liquor and prostitutes had been concerns of city officials as early as the 1860s. Seventeen saloons existed in 1867 at the height of the railroad boom, twelve in the doldrums of 1874. "Camp-following" women were present in even larger numbers. Sometimes they were chased beyond the city limits, but business was so lucrative that they simply set up tents in the fields until the self-righteous citizenry tired of the crusade. Historian John Jeffries has concluded that a policy of peaceful coexistence was in effect most of the time, "unless interrupted by violence."[66]

City officials faced a crisis over liquor in 1880 when Kansas legislators voted to make the entire state "dry." One issue was simply loss of revenue, because saloon licensing at $200 a year per establishment had become an important way to finance local government.[67] Another problem was the realization that unregulated bootleggers soon would proliferate around the post and thereby create social difficulties much greater than had existed before. The result was a practical, though technically illegal, solution. A succession of mayors and town councils, all running on the Liberal ticket, decided to regulate rather than eliminate what they came to call "resorts." They promptly closed ones that were poorly managed, citing the letter of the state law. Other saloons faced only occasional fines for their transgressions, however, with the amounts being set at approximately the same level as the former licensing fee. As editor George Martin summed up the thinking, you "weed two-thirds of them out, and make the balance support the city. A fool sentiment must ultimately give way to common sense."[68]

The system of saloon regulation in Junction City included an important geographical element. Raucous but still allowable establishments were permitted only on the northern fringe of downtown. This was the Bowery district near the depot. At the other end of the spectrum, a few select drinking establishments that catered to the local business elite, distinguished visitors, and Fort Riley officers were allowed near the Bartell House (see map 3). There were three in 1905: the Capitol at 523 North Washington (see fig. 20), the Senate at 601, and the Midland at 603. In addition, the Bartell itself discreetly maintained a basement bar with a separate, outside entrance. Finally, middle-status saloons were given free rein between Eighth and Ninth Streets on Washington. None of this zonation was written down as official canon, of course, but it was real enough by 1896 for Judge O. L. Moore to uphold an injunction that kept a new saloon from opening in the northern portion of the 600-block. He stated simply that it had long been city policy "that neither the saloon or the bawdy house shall encroach further upon Washington Street."[69]

Because saloons operated openly in Junction City, their owners occasionally asked Pennell for his services, just as did other merchants. His photographs of the Senate and the Horseshoe display a contrast in social status (figs. 37 and 38). The Senate, run by Alfred York and Peter Volz, was described by the *Union* as having not only "the very best brands of beer, wines, liquors, and cigars" but also a reputation that was "above reproach." Another measure of its prestige was that a group of people who gathered for regular talk down the street at the Sargent Drug Store called themselves "the Coca-Cola Senate."[70] At the Horseshoe, one of six saloons in the 800-block of North Washington, a visitor would find a workingman's crowd. Its bar was still quite elaborate, but neither of its bartenders wore a vest for the photograph, and the floor covering showed considerable wear. The screening visible between the barroom proper and the outside world was standard for all saloons. It protected customers from the sometimes prying eyes of passersby.

Prostitution received even less newspaper coverage than did saloons. Scattered accounts, however, suggest a concentration at the Bowery with an extension onto East Ninth Street. Ninth Street was to become a center for nightlife and African American business in the 1920s, but it contained no commercial buildings during the Pennell years. The women must have worked out of private residences or boarding houses. Like saloons, Junction City brothels operated openly but had to follow a series of strict though unwritten laws concerning geography, finance, and social mores. The job of enforcing these edicts—as well as dealing with the many other ticklish incidents that occurred daily, when the desires of 1,500 or so soldiers meshed uneasily with those of several thousand local citizens—fell to the town marshal. This position required the talents of a special man. For over thirty years, Tom Allen Cullinan achieved legendary status in the role (fig. 39).[71]

It may surprise some people that Pennell photographed several prostitutes, but they were businesspeople too. Some of the women wanted prints for their own use, others to sell to customers as souvenirs (figs. 40 and 41). No details exist on the lives of Nellie Martin, Madame Sperber, or any of the other women in these two photographs. George Martin, in relating a story about Marshal Cullinan, provides one vivid example of the social rules that were applied to the group in the early 1880s:

> In those days Junction City was noted for the famous hostelry of Madam Blue, who had statesmen do her homage—she was a Swede, smart, and a "beaut"—and her name appeared in fifth district and legislative politics. To all appearances the house was as quiet and orderly as a house could be. Tom was mighty particular in suppressing signs of lewdness on the streets. His watch-tower was generally in front of the Bartell House, while south, on the opposite side, in the next block, was the madam's resort. A fresh or green girl came to town and put up at the madam's. In the evening she was out swinging on the front gate. Tom walked over and informed her that that was not allowed; that if she wanted to play she must go in the back yard. She did it a second night and he stopped her; she did it a third night, when Tom went into the house, found her trunk in a second-story room, threw it out the window, sash and glass, into the street, and made her go down to the depot and wait for a train.[72]

37. The Senate, 1899 (print 468.16). Indicators of quality abound in this "resort": a magnificent hand-carved wooden bar, an expensive lighting fixture, and cut-glass squares above the mirrors. Stemware stacked on the back bar is for serving wine. Note also the sign that proves that Anheuser-Busch has been in business for over a century.

38. The Horseshoe, 1906 (print 1774). Reflected in the mirror is the name Blatz, one of the beers sold here. More interesting, perhaps, is the police badge worn by one of the customers. He has been tentatively identified as Officer King, and the middle patron at the bar as Charles Sipperly (*Junction City Union,* July 14, 1975). A reminder of this bar's location remained long after it had closed—a small terrazzo horseshoe embedded in the sidewalk at 805 North Washington. This particular photograph also lives in the land of television reruns, for it is shown in the opening credits of *Cheers,* a popular series from the 1980s and 1990s.

40. Nellie Martin (left) and friend, 1905 (print 1612). A staid Edwardian background of rug and wallpaper design, pastoral painting, and piano contrasts with the foreground of beer, playing cards, and loose-fitting garments in a manner that is perhaps deliberate. No rings grace these fingers.

39 (opposite). Thomas Allen Cullinan, 1901 (print 740). Cullinan (1838–1904), known to everyone as Tom Allen, became a folk hero while serving as the city marshal of Junction City between 1871 and 1904. As George Martin put it: "He enforced the law in his own way, with the hearty approval of the entire population. That is, if Tom Allen deemed it proper, he could take a man before the police court, or lock him up, and it was all right; if he deemed it proper to administer the law by walloping the earth with a loafer, that too was deemed all right. He could smell a criminal the moment he touched the townsite, and he had a remarkably effective way of telling them to leave town" (*Kansas Historical Collections* 9 [1905–1906]: 536).

41. Madame Sperber group, 1906 (print 1720). Worn linoleum suggests a poorer setting for this brothel than the one glimpsed in figure 40, but the clothing of both sets of women is similar. The dresses are short, but all legs are fully covered. Dark puffs on the slippers of the two women on the left look identical to those worn by Nellie Martin's friend.

The brothel and saloon businesses in Junction City underwent a series of major changes between 1901 and 1906. First, in February 1901, federal officials declared that liquor would no longer be served on post.[73] Traffic promptly boomed in town, leading to financial gains that were coupled with increased social problems. Local leaders overlooked the difficulties initially, but some of them changed their minds in 1902, when a portion of the Tenth Cavalry was transferred to Fort Riley for a year's stay. Many more locals protested in 1904, when a larger group of about 250 soldiers from the Ninth Cavalry came to the fort. These concerns were racial, because both of the regiments in question were African American.

Although Junction City would later establish a relatively enlightened policy of tolerance in matters racial and ethnic, this first experience was hostile. Most of the trouble was soldier versus soldier, and some of the worst clashes took place off-post in Junction City's various "resorts."[74] Resolution came about through an unofficial policy of segregation, with Madame Sperber's operation being one beneficiary. Unfortunately for her, however, the Ninth Cavalry was transferred away in early 1907, and Fort Riley once again became racially homogeneous. The frightening brawls from 1904 and 1905 turned some people's minds against the whole idea of saloons. In this way, they helped prepare the city for a huge and unexpected cultural and financial blow that came in late 1906. Kansas attorney general C. C. Coleman filed suit against the local governments of Junction City, Atchison, Pittsburg, and Kansas City for open violation of the prohibitory law. The news stunned local officials, but they decided not to protest. Literally overnight, an age came to an end.[75]

The Economic Base: Agriculture, Mills, and Railroads

If a person relies only on newspaper accounts for local history, it is easy to be persuaded that townspeople, through entrepreneurial zeal, created their own successes. Boosterism was and is important to development, but such a focus overlooks more fundamental underpinnings of the economy. During the Pennell years, Fort Riley contributed by far the largest number of dollars that found their way into the stores along Washington Street. It was joined by three other basic, but less heralded, industries: farming, milling, and railroading.

Geary, partly because it possesses the second-smallest area of any county in Kansas, has never received statewide acclaim for its agriculture. This anonymity is also a product of diversity. Its eastern townships are part of the magnificent grazing country known as the Flint Hills. Most of the western acreage, in contrast, consists of either flat uplands suitable for wheat or rich bottomlands along the Republican and Smoky Hill Rivers and the smaller Lyon and Clark's Creeks (see map 1). The total impact of farming was substantial, however. The county's field crops carried a value of over $1 million in the 1905 state census, and animals and animal products sold for a half million more.

Pennell did not cart his bulky camera equipment into the countryside often, but he nevertheless managed to capture much of the character of rural life. Of the nearly 900 farms in the county, the most typical ones centered on an isolated house and barn set in a sea of upland grass (fig. 42). These enterprises had no one specialty. Chickens and perhaps a few pigs would roam around the farmstead proper, with pasture and wheat on the uplands and some corn in

42. Geary County farmstead, 1902 (print 940). Given the rigidity of the weekly cycle of household chores, the presence of washing on the clothesline means that this photograph almost surely was taken on a Monday. The season was fall rather than spring, judging from the condition of the road. Note the rock wall behind the wagon. It was not an aesthetic indulgence but rather a practical way to utilize stones that had to be removed from this and many other upland fields. In contrast, the telephone wires that run along the road are most unusual, because home service was only partially available in town in 1902. The lines likely are long-distance connectors to either Abilene or Topeka.

the best lowland fields. Nearly every family tended an orchard as well, such as the young trees set near the road on the right side of the photograph. The house type shown is typical, too. Called an I-house because of its prevalence in Illinois, Indiana, and Iowa, the design has cultural origins in southeastern Pennsylvania. Four rooms constitute its main section. Often, as here, people would add a kitchen ell on the back side.

Corn was the crop of choice in Geary County wherever it could be grown, because none of the small grains could match its potential for generating dollars per acre. Local farmers planted 51,661 acres to corn in 1905, compared with only 17,946 to wheat, and from these they harvested 1,653,152 bushels worth over $595,000. During this period, long before people bought hybrid varieties from specialized dealers, each farmer would carefully select his or her own seed from the best ears of the previous year. Skill was involved, and the competition for highest yields and tallest plants was keen. Merchants in Junction City cashed in on the spirit by sponsoring an annual corn-growing contest for boys and, in 1907, by holding a special corn carnival.[76] Sometimes a proud man would call a photographer out to document the results (fig. 43).

Second to corn in agricultural value was cattle. Local farmers owned nearly 25,000 of these animals in 1905, about 86 percent of which were raised for beef rather than milk. Several hundred of these beeves found a direct market every year in town at the Junction City Packing Company. Frank D. Coryell and Hale Powers had opened this business in 1904 as a means of supplying their own and other local butcher shops (see map 2).[77] Most of the county's animals were shipped by rail to Kansas City, however, and many of these passed through the stockyards of Thomas Dixon (fig. 44).

Wheat, the third important leg of Geary County agriculture, provided the single most dramatic event in the seasonal cycle of rural life: threshing. In midsummer, hugely powerful and proportionately loud steam-traction engines would emerge from their sheds to drive even larger machines that somehow could delicately separate grain from chaff. Threshing in this way was a revolutionary experience that had begun to replace simpler horse-powered separators in the 1880s. It introduced a world of oil and steel into a community that was used to manure and wood. It brought excitement, tension, and, for women, the challenge of feeding a crew of ten or more hungry men.[78] By the turn of the century, Pennell had joined nearly every other photographer of his day in trying to capture the clamor of this spectacle.

Threshing equipment in the age of steam was far too expensive and used too infrequently for individual farmers to own. Instead, specialists arose who would buy the machinery, recruit a crew, and offer their packaged services for hire. C. J. Olson, George Schmultz, and Peter Gfeller formed one such company at Alida in 1899, about five miles northwest of Junction City (fig. 45). The equipment they purchased was a year old, but the separator had all the latest options: a blower (to disperse the straw), a self-feeder (a conveyor system), and a self-measurer (to record the amount of grain threshed). The *Union* reported new records for the group day after day, culminating in an output of 1,534 bushels for a single morning's work, despite moving the engine twice and the separator four times.[79]

Details of the threshing process are better seen from a different visual perspective (fig. 46). Steam tractors are massive machines. Weighing between ten and twenty tons each, they broke

43. Andrew Engstrom's cornfield, 1914 (print 2731). Engstrom lived near Dwight, in southeastern Geary County. His field probably was in the valley of either Dry or Humboldt Creek. Judging from the spacing of the ladder steps, the corn is approximately thirteen feet tall. This height dwarfs current varieties but was far from the Kansas record of twenty-two feet, four inches reported near Downs (*Junction City Union,* September 1, 1899).

44. Dixon stockyards, 1902 (print 834). Thomas Dixon (1831–1899) owned a 1,280-acre farm and ranch north of Ogden and became wealthy through a series of contracts to supply Fort Riley with hay, wood, flour, and beef. In 1879 he built a combination elevator and stockyard near the corner of Fifth and Monroe (*Junction City Union,* April 17, 1899). It was a small but efficient operation. A single Hereford, a breed that was beginning to dominate Flint Hills pastures, looks at the camera. Behind are a series of holding pens (wooden, to protect nervous animals) and a loading chute that leads directly into a stock car. The barn is for hay storage, the wooden platform in the foreground for weighing loads.

45. Alida threshing company, 1899 (print 468.3). Workers had specialized duties on a threshing crew. Among those pictured are Toby Meyers, who ran the steam engine; his assistants George Schmultz and H. C. Geist, who hauled water and coal, respectively; George McCrumber, the cook; and pitchers C. A. Geist, Crist Weitrich, Frank Kesserman, G. Melki, and Christ Eislie, who loaded shocks onto wagons and then fed them into the big stationary separator (*Junction City Union,* September 8, 1899). All are young. Two straw piles flank the engine. The large tube jutting forward is a wind stacker, which ejects the straw.

46. Threshing in Tom Dixon's wheat field, 1913 (print 2648). The field behind the wagons is dotted with shocks. Workers would load these onto specially designed bundle wagons equipped with racks for holding their bulky cargo. The wagons then would be positioned beside the self-feeder on the threshing machine as shown, taking care not to interfere with the power belt. A separator man, standing atop his machine, oversees the pitching of shocks onto the feeder ramp and occasionally rotates the wind stacker that is creating the straw pile. Grain wagons stand ready near the far end of the separator to receive the bulk wheat. This engine burns coal, but some were designed to use straw as a fuel.

many a wooden bridge as they lumbered from farm to farm at a rate of two or three miles per hour. They were hazardous in other ways as well. The seeming inefficiency of having their power belts routinely extend some fifty feet to the separator was a precaution to lessen the risk of sparks setting fire to a straw pile. Every community also had at least one tale of a boiler explosion. Junction City's took place in September 1909 at the Schuler farm, twelve miles southwest of town. Engineer Otto Kruger was killed instantly, his body "hurled through the air for a distance of sixty feet." G. E. Martin, his water hauler, suffered two broken legs, and two other men were badly burned.[80]

Farmers in western Kansas used the big steam-traction machines with some success to plow their fields, but they were heavy, slow, and wasteful of fuel. A lighter gasoline-powered version would be needed if ordinary farmers were ever to replace their horses. Such a development lagged behind that of automobiles, but a few of these more mobile traction engines began to appear in Geary County in 1911. Peter Gfeller, who farmed near Upland in adjacent Dickinson County, was one of the pioneers (fig. 47), and the Muenzenmayer Hardware Company sold early models to Jacob Heer and W. Zuricke. By 1915, as men and horses began to be drawn off the farm and into the war effort, the popularity of tractors (as they were now called) was increasing rapidly. A reporter estimated that county farmers now owned a hundred of them and predicted that the machines would plow virtually all the fields that coming fall.[81]

Flour mills, like stockyards and packing plants, were a means of integrating farm and town life in Junction City. They also had the potential to be important contributors to the economy, and many early writers had seen a bright future for the community as a milling center. Wheat was nearby, as were railroads to ship the product, and the water power was excellent. Cornelius Fogarty agreed with this assessment. In 1874 he selected a site on the Smoky Hill just east of town. There, where the river hugged Grand View Bluff, he installed a dam nine feet high and erected a classic stone mill (fig. 48). His business was said to be the first west of Topeka, and he prospered over the years, managing to adapt easily to the transitions from soft to hard varieties of wheat and from local to statewide and regional markets.[82]

Although Fogarty could and did modify his mill to match the changing times, the water power that had prompted his original site selection eventually proved to be a major liability. Newer mills positioned themselves directly beside railroad tracks to ensure efficient shipping. They also powered their rollers with large steam engines whose work could not be interrupted by ice or inadequate stream flow. This new conception of a mill first appeared in Junction City in 1893 when D. Waldo Tyler arrived from South Dakota to construct Aurora Mills (fig. 49). Tyler located his mill on Eighth Street, just east of the Union Pacific and MKT tracks (see map 2). Although his daily grinding capacity of 250 barrels was only marginally greater than that of Fogarty, his efficiency was far higher. An attached elevator that held 50,000 bushels, for example, ensured him a relatively constant supply of grain.[83]

The movement of local mills from river to railroad was completed in 1905. Four years after Fogarty's death and a month after the Smoky Hill temporarily washed out his dam, Fogarty's nephew and heir, Thomas Hogan, announced that he would build a new facility even larger than Aurora Mills. He, too, selected a site on East Eighth and contracted with Ziegler and

47. Peter Gfeller's tractor, 1911 (print 2393). Gfeller, who specialized in the production of Angus beef cattle, was an early adopter of both the automobile and the tractor. This model is a Minneapolis Universal 20-40, manufactured by the Minneapolis Threshing Machine Company. It has a two-cylinder engine, weighs about 5,000 pounds, and presumably was more than capable of pulling the five-bottom disc plow attached to it. Metal wheels, with lugs on the rear, were standard on early tractors. These worked fine in fields but could damage many road surfaces. The barn also reveals Gfeller's progressive nature. Designs that allowed hay to be loaded into the loft from the outside with a hook-and-pulley system became common in Kansas only after 1900. Flanking the proud owner are his son, Emil, and a grandson.

48. Fogarty's mill, 1900 (print 582). Cornelius Fogarty commissioned this photograph to record a series of improvements to his mill: a new fourth story and mansard roof, an elevator addition (the ell on the downstream side), and a new separator and scourer inside (*Junction City Union,* September 8, 1899). The bridge on the right was the only route east from town and carried heavy traffic. Besides his milling business, Fogarty also provided the first electricity for Junction City. Wires for this purpose are visible above the dam.

49. Aurora Mills, 1913 (print 2588). Eight buildings form the mill complex. The engine room on the left initially held a 120-horsepower, coal-powered steam generator. This was later replaced with a larger model of the same type and then, in 1906, with a cleaner oil burner. The tall, metal-clad elevator to the right of the main building has a capacity of 50,000 bushels of wheat. Two airtight steel tanks, each thirty feet in diameter, stand at the far end of the row. They were added in 1898 to provide additional storage capacity (*Junction City Union,* September 2, 1898; July 20, 1900; January 22, 1904; May 6, 1906).

Dalton for a five-story stone structure. The completed mill, which drew praise for its grandeur, could produce 500 barrels of flour each day and featured electrical power rather than steam. From the perspective of a railroad engineer or any traveler from the east, the two facilities came to dominate the city skyline (fig. 50).[84]

Before Fort Riley was designated as a permanent installation and began the massive construction program that would sweep the economy of Junction City upward, town officials had courted railroads and railroad facilities with enthusiasm. After the Fort Riley development, however, a more casual attitude prevailed. The city actually secured two major employment coups from the Union Pacific during these years, but the timing of these events was such that they were not fully appreciated by many townspeople. The first one, the movement of the division point from Wamego to Junction City, took place in 1889, in the midst of the big construction at Fort Riley. The second, the erection of major shop facilities in 1917, was overshadowed by waves of soldiers coming to the fort as the United States entered World War I.

Junction City leaders had little to do with making their town the headquarters for the Union Pacific's first division west from Kansas City. Basically, it was a matter of better designs for railroad engines. Because newer locomotives could travel farther between servicings, company officials decided in 1889 that they could eliminate their old second division, headquartered at Brookville. They simply moved the first changeover for crews westward from Wamego another thirty miles or so. For Junction City, this meant an influx of 150 brakemen, conductors, engineers, and firemen, plus 70 or so mechanics and laborers. These employees translated into a population increase for the town of at least 500, and a monthly payroll of between $8,000 and $9,000.[85]

When the railroad awarded the division point to Junction City, it was rumored that the Union Pacific's equally lucrative major repair shops soon would follow. These facilities had always been located in Kansas City, but the site there was old, cramped, and increasingly off-center for the railroad as a whole. George A. Rockwell, one of the town's leading businessmen, headed an effort to ensure that Junction City was selected for this prize instead of Lawrence, Manhattan, or other possible bidders (fig. 51). He achieved apparent success in 1907 when the railroad company purchased a 300-acre site near the intersection between the main line and the Fort Kearney branch (see map 2) and announced plans to build. Construction was unexpectedly delayed, however, not just for a few months but for several years. Pessimists assumed the worst, but all turned out well. The company accepted bids in September 1917 for a $2 million facility.[86]

The new Union Pacific shops meant another 200 jobs when they finally opened in late 1919. The buildings included a twenty-stall roundhouse, a large brick and steel machine shop, a new coaling station, and a 200,000-gallon water tank (figs. 52 and 53). Few communities in Kansas could now match Junction City as a railroad town. It was home to over 400 employees on the main line, another 15 or so on the Fort Kearney branch, and about 30 on the MKT.[87]

50. Coal car, 1908 (print 2084). The tracks of the MKT and the Union Pacific paralleled each other through Junction City. This view looks south, with Pennell standing near Twelfth Street. The Union Pacific tracks and depot are on the right. A pair of metal grain tanks marks Aurora Mills, while the newer and taller Hogan Star Mills looms over the depot. Coal, the fuel of choice in American homes at the time, was a major freight item on all rail lines.

51. George A. Rockwell family, 1913 (print 2653). George A. (1854–1930) was the younger brother of Bertrand Rockwell. He took over management of the family store in 1907 when Bertrand retired and moved to Kansas City. Standing to the left of Rockwell and his wife, Annie, are their sons George C., a career army officer, and Walter, who was the last Rockwell to run the store. Standing on the right are Annie Rockwell's sister, Florence Coleman, and the third son, Frank E., who worked as a mining engineer. The three adults in the front, left to right, are Cecil, the wife of Walter; Virginia, the only daughter of George A. and Annie; and Mary, the wife of Frank. Robert A., the son of Frank, is at the bottom left, followed across by David, the son of Walter; George C., Jr.; and Jane, a daughter of Walter. The family home at 324 North Jefferson stands in the background.

52. Union Pacific roundhouse and shops, 1920 (print 3301). Roundhouses, huge and drafty buildings, were where workers performed routine maintenance on locomotives. This one was 20 feet high, 99 feet deep, and over 550 feet from side to side. A circular turntable, shown in front, was used to direct engines into the appropriate bays, as well as to turn them around when finished. The two-story machine shop sits behind and to the right of the roundhouse. These facilities at Junction City supplemented, but did not replace, those in Kansas City.

53. Union Pacific engine, 1911 (print 2453). Steam locomotives are classified by the number and arrangement of their wheels. This model is a 4-6-0 (a pilot truck of four wheels at the front, six large drive wheels, and no following truck under the cab). Small 4-4-0 engines predominated on midwestern railroads in the 1880s, and big 2-12-2s in the 1930s and 1940s. A 4-6-0 (often referred to as a ten-wheeler) had excellent balance but was considered underpowered by the time of this photograph. Engine 1437 probably was seeing duty on the branch line between Junction City and Concordia. It is shown in front of the old roundhouse.

The Economic Base: Fort Riley

The Fort Riley that General Sheridan began to create in the late 1880s was to have multiple purposes. Writers often referred to it as the great central camp of the nation. With almost 20,000 acres, it was much larger than other posts of the time and therefore physically capable of replacing numerous small installations that soon would be abandoned in the region. For training maneuvers, it could hold "almost any number" of troops. The heart of the institution, however, was to be a pair of permanent, interconnected schools for soldiers in the cavalry and light artillery service. The original intent was for a depot to train all young recruits in these areas, but by the time the initial construction had been completed, the focus had been switched to the training of more advanced officers and enlisted men.[88]

As army planners looked over the small collection of barracks, corrals, and other buildings that constituted the post in the mid-1880s, they saw mostly poorly constructed, undersized frame structures, all in sad repair. Consequently, they instructed Captain George E. Pond, the new quartermaster who arrived in September 1885, to create a virtually new post on the old site. The material was to be native limestone, the designs classic, and the quality high.[89]

Captain Pond took bids for the initial set of barracks and three officers' quarters in October 1886. These would house cavalry units. A few months later came the authorization for five additional officers' quarters, including one for the post commander. Pond then turned his attention to the artillery school. He selected a site adjacent to the cavalry unit across a small ravine to the east, laid out a second parade ground, and, in September 1887, took bids for sixteen buildings. Things continued at a pace only slightly less hectic for several years. Pond built stables and additional barracks and quarters. He added a hospital and mess hall in 1888, an academic building in 1889, and a riding hall in 1891. Then, with the basic elements all in place, the formal order came early in 1892 to open the new school.[90]

Approximately 1,000 soldiers were stationed at Fort Riley during the early Pennell years. Typically these included four troops of cavalry (400 men), three batteries of light artillery (510 men), and a band (25 men), plus 10 or so noncommissioned officers and hospital staff and about 50 regular officers. Together they infused both the post and Junction City with incredible energy. Over 500 local civilians worked on the various big construction projects, and an ongoing series of contracts to furnish the post with food and supplies boded well for the future. The hay concession for 1906 alone was worth $34,000, and the one for oats $100,000. Even more important to local merchants was the annual soldiers' payroll of nearly a half million dollars. No wonder the three miles of road between town and post were well maintained.[91]

For the generations of contemporary Kansans used to Interstate Highway 70, it may come as a surprise to learn that the main road into Junction City for most of its history passed through Fort Riley (fig. 54). This route, which came to be known as Grant Avenue, was an extension of an old military connector with Fort Leavenworth. It paralleled the Union Pacific tracks for most of its length, joined with Eighteenth Street just beyond the city limits, and then intersected with Washington Street (see map 2). A traveler to the fort from Junction City on this route would first cross over the Republican River and floodplain. Then, after ascending a small escarpment and passing by the post cemetery and hay storage area, he or she

54. Grant Avenue, 1898–1899 (print 390.11). Because an estimated 65 percent of travelers into Junction City used the Fort Riley road, including soldiers with paychecks in hand, city officials maintained it well. They spent $13,000 in 1891 to create an all-weather macadam surface. Three years later, they lined the route with trees (*Junction City Union,* July 9, 1909).

would arrive at the cavalry school (map 4). This place, the site of the original post and the heart of the reconceived one, was roughly triangular and was bordered by small ravines on the northwest and northeast. It focused on a central parade field, with officers' quarters on the north side and barracks for the enlisted men on the south (fig. 55). A dozen stables tucked away behind the barracks marked the limit of the elevated land. From these stables, soldiers would hear a series of predictable clicks and whistles from Union Pacific trains as they passed nearby along the edge of the floodplain. These sounds, in fact, were so regular and familiar that they provided a useful supplement to the bugle as a means of marking time.

Every part of the reconstituted cavalry grounds at Fort Riley exuded quality, a trait not surprising for the most elite branch of the army.[92] This refinement was most apparent along Forsyth Avenue, where housing for senior officers had been concentrated (fig. 56). By the turn of the century, after the new landscape plantings had matured a little, the overall appearance of the post prompted many visitors to wax poetic. One account from the *Topeka Mail and Breeze* compared it to an upper-class urban residential area:

> It is the most beautiful little city I have ever visited. The houses are all of stone, the lawns are all of blue grass and are just like broad green velvet carpets. The streets and sidewalks are almost clean enough to eat from. Not a twig, not a dead leaf, not a stray stone is allowed out of its place. The long avenues lined with trees are perfect pictures of natural beauty. The officers' quarters are roomy and are usually three-story buildings. A steam plant, said to be the largest in the United States, and probably in the world, has a heating radius more extensive than any in the domain of Uncle Sam. Every building is comfortable, and heated from the same head.[93]

The most important building on any cavalry post was the riding hall. Fort Riley's turreted version was a heavy yet spacious structure. It stood 300 feet long and 100 feet wide and was constructed without any interior support posts (figs. 57 and 58). Each troop and battery would come here with their mounts for daily training during the winter months. Periods of sixty to ninety minutes each were rotated among the various units, but this was never enough for a group of men devoted to horses and horsemanship. Although their hall already was the biggest one in the service, Fort Riley officers began to push for additional facilities almost as soon as the last mortar had dried on the original 1891 structure. Their efforts were rewarded in 1906 with an appropriation of $60,000 for a second building. Called the West Riding Hall, the new model relied more on structural steel for its support than did the older facility. It could therefore have more and larger windows for better natural light (fig. 59). The two halls made the post the envy of every military horseman, and it is probably no coincidence that Fort Riley officers began to win medals regularly at national horse shows.[94]

Young men were said to have joined the cavalry during the 1890s because of some combination of a love for horses and a romanticized view of medieval knights or dashing Indian fighters. They were not disappointed as far as the horses were concerned. Instruction at the school involved up to seven and a half hours in the saddle daily, except during the winter months. Few textbooks existed, but this was of small concern. Instructors thought that students learned best through a series of practical exercises. Mornings always were spent with the horses, either at the stables or in various mounted drills (figs. 60 and 61). Afternoons were mainly for classroom exercises, fatigue duty, and athletics (figs. 62 and 63).[95]

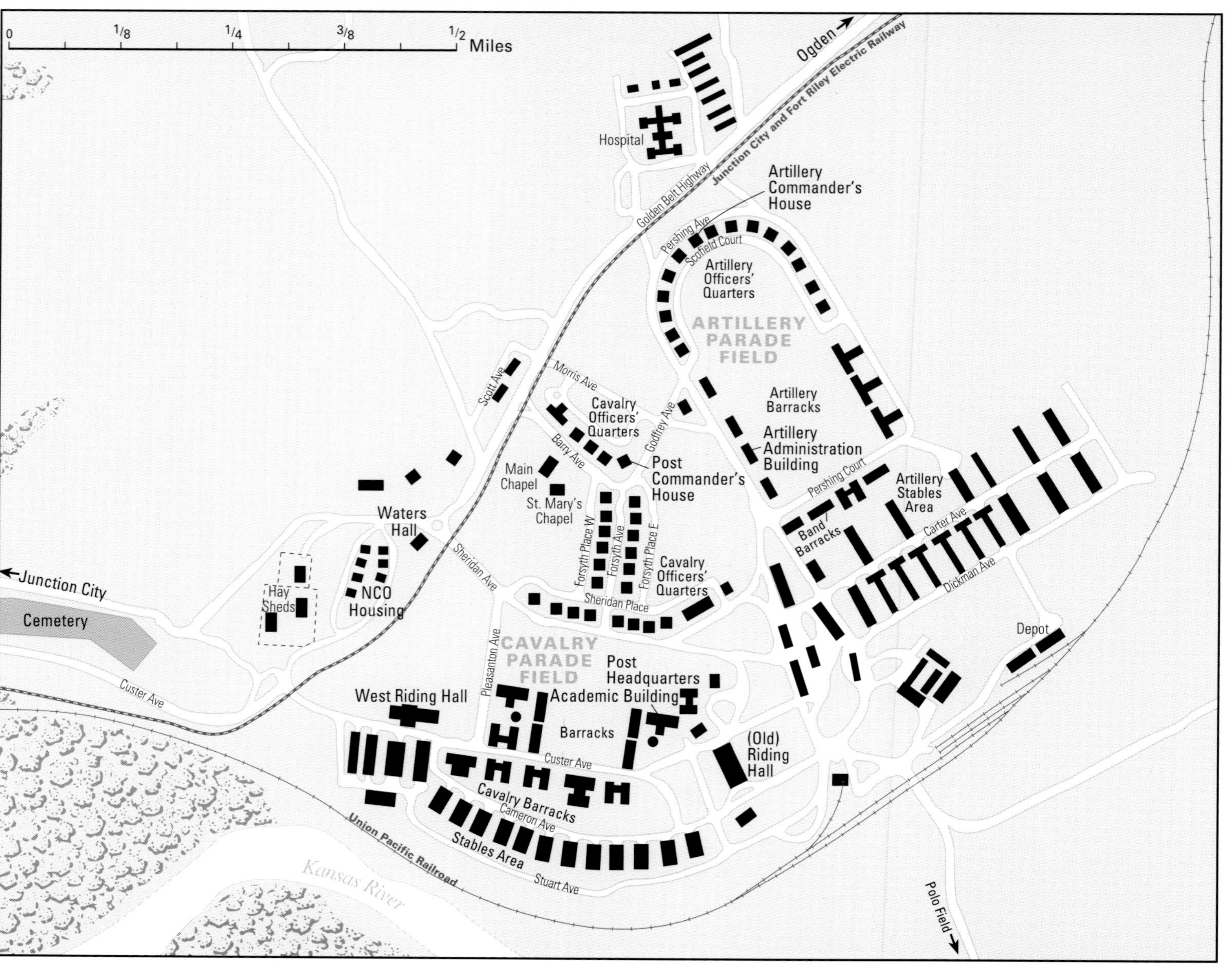

Map 4. Fort Riley Reference Map, circa 1915

55. Cavalry parade field, 1900 (print 571.1). The large twin barracks at the edge of the parade field date from 1887 and were the first buildings erected during the reconstruction of Fort Riley. Each housed 136 men. The post hospital, built in 1888, is the towered structure on the left. Practicing on the field is the Sixth Cavalry Band. This was a unit set apart from the regular cavalry, a full-time job for two dozen or so men. They played often in Junction City, traveled to smaller posts, and did much to promote goodwill.

56. Forsyth Place East, 1895 (print 16.5). Forsyth Avenue and its flanking streets, Forsyth Place East and West, are the site of twelve duplexes built for cavalry officers and their families between 1887 and 1894. Their name honors James W. Forsyth, the commander of the post during the construction years. He initiated a series of reforms regarding alcohol abuse by soldiers and unauthorized grazing on reservation property by civilian cattle. Note the cement (not limestone) sidewalk and the newness of the tree plantings.

57. Riding hall, 1895 (print 13.13). The Junction City firm of Ziegler and Dalton constructed this building in 1891. That contract became a springboard for landing over $5 million worth of similar work at Forts Ethan Allen, Sam Houston, Sill, and other posts across the country (*Junction City Union,* April 10, 1913).

58. Gibbs in the riding hall, 1897 (print 161). Gibbs was a member of the Second Cavalry, Troop A. He apparently had recovered well from a fight earlier in the year at Junction City. His severed wrist arteries required two hours to repair, but Gibbs filed no complaint (*Junction City Union,* February 12, 1897). Training a horse to lie down on command was more than just amusement. It might enable a soldier to escape detection in open country and could provide him with an emergency shield. Note that although the riding hall was spacious, it was not well lit. Upon construction of a second facility, this original one became known as the East Riding Hall.

59. West Riding Hall, 1914 (print 2727). Just as they had done sixteen years earlier, Ziegler and Dalton won the contract to build Fort Riley's second riding hall in 1907. It was the final major project for the firm. Located just southwest of the parade field, the new hall was even more expansive than the older one: 100 feet by 333 feet. On the floor are four of the many varieties of jumps used in mounted drills.

60. Trooper at the stables, 1909 (print 2178). Cavalrymen were trained to be meticulous about posture as well as the care of horses and equipment. They were especially proud of their McClellan saddles, a service tradition since 1858. McClellans were light in weight and designed to carry a grain bag in front and a tent behind. A boot held the soldier's rifle on the left side, and his saber attached to the pommel on the right. Leather hoods on the stirrups protected against cold and brush (Truscott, *Twilight,* pp. 20–22). This view looks to the east. The main row of stables is on the right; the old (east) riding hall stands in the left background.

61. Captain Walter C. Short and officers, 1905 (print 1441.4). Cavalry officers had a reputation for immaculate personal appearance. Captain Short, of the Sixth Cavalry, served a long tour of duty at Fort Riley. He was in charge of a new school established for farriers in 1903 and then became senior instructor in the Department of Equitation and Horse Training. In 1910, he was named assistant commandant of the post. The group is posed in front of the original riding hall.

62. Dissecting a horse, 1916 (print 2858). Besides mounted drills, students in the mounted-service school took classroom courses on tactics, drill regulations, topography, equitation and horse training, horseshoeing, and hippology (Pride, *History of Fort Riley,* p. 236). Anatomy instruction was part of the program in hippology.

63. Supper in camp, 1897 (print 141.8). Because cavalry life often involved time patrolling in isolated areas, field skills were important. All soldiers learned how to construct brush arbors for shelter. Partly to the same end, a special school for cooks and bakers was established at Fort Riley in 1905 under the direction of Captain M. S. Murray (Pride, *History of Fort Riley,* p. 239).

The terrain of the Fort Riley reservation, grassy but with wooded patches and dissected near the rivers into a complex series of ravines and small canyons, was ideal for the instruction of military riding skills. Cavalrymen loved the place. Years afterward they could still tick off the place names automatically, especially those that had most tested their skills: "Three Mile Creek, Packers Camp, Wolf, Coyote, Magazine, Pumphouse, Rock Spring, Governor Harvey, and Breakneck canyons."[96] More than a few veterans even went back to relive their experiences. One took along his son, a wide-eyed fifteen-year-old, who later recalled the high adventure:

> For three days they relived their days as both students and instructors by taking me as their new "student" on every wild ride they had ever been on in those earlier years: in and out of all the canyons; down all of the slides; fording and then swimming the Republican River, in the water holding on to the horse's tail and being pulled along behind him; over every type of jump known to man; galloping wildly through the mounted pistol course, the saber course, and the course that was a combination of the two; dashing through a modified stakes course; and finally a two-hour night ride rather than the six or eight of their earlier years. When it was all over they informed me that I was the only man to graduate from the Advanced Equitation Course in three days, but only because of the high quality of the instructors, not the ability of the student.[97]

The artillery post at Fort Riley, although often housing more men than the cavalry barracks, existed in the shadow of the mounted unit. The chief cavalry officer was always the commander of the fort as a whole, and local newspaper coverage was heavily biased in the same way. The artillerymen could take solace, however, in having a beautifully designed complex of buildings and grounds. Everything was stone, of course, and the look classically formal. A semicircular drive lined with officers' quarters set the tone (see map 4). The ends of this semicircle extended to the south, where they enclosed a handsome parade field and provided sites for barracks and other buildings along their flanks (fig. 64). Farther south, beyond the ends of the drive, a series of stables overlooked the river bottoms and the Union Pacific tracks, as did those of the cavalry.

The numerous stables at the artillery post served as a reminder that the interests of these soldiers overlapped greatly with those of their neighbors across the small ravine. Field artillery frequently supported cavalrymen in battle, and the guns, although powerful, were designed to be fully portable (figs. 65 and 66). Horses pulled these machines, of course, so artillerymen enrolled in hippology classes along with the cavalry students.

Junction City people did not distinguish much between artillery and cavalry personnel. In contrast, they clearly did so between enlisted men and officers. Enlistees were overwhelmingly young (often still in their teens), energetic, and single. Being so, they naturally sought releases from their regimented lives whenever possible (fig. 67). Some of this came through athletics, some through gambling. The saloon in Waters Hall also was heavily used before the War Department closed it down in 1901 (fig. 68). Watchful eyes and bartenders forbidden to serve customers who showed signs of intoxication limited the appeal of the post canteen, however, so soldiers regularly went farther afield. They staged parties on outlying portions of the reservation, usually well supplied with bootleg liquor (fig. 69).[98] They also visited area towns: Ogden, Manhattan, and even Kansas City. The most common recreational destination, of course, was nearby Junction City with its brightly lit stores, comforting bars, and attractive

64. Artillery administration building, 1895 (print 13.8). Constructed in 1889, the administration building contained an auditorium that served as the principal classroom for early student soldiers. Pennell took this photograph while standing on the artillery parade field. Parts of the cavalry campus are visible in the left background, including the riding hall and the top of the hospital tower.

65. Captain Potts and his battery at Pawnee Flats, 1899 (print 468.14). A battery is the artillery equivalent to a troop in the cavalry or a company in the infantry. Each contains 100 to 150 men. The number of horses in the photograph exceeds the number of guns, an indication that "light artillery" is only a relative term. This setting, Pawnee Flats, is part of the Kansas River valley about two miles northeast of the main post. An example of the wooded ravines valued for cavalry training is in the distance.

66. Second Battery gun squad, 1907 (print 1881.1). The U.S. Army defines artillery as any gun that uses ammunition greater than one inch in diameter and that is not fired from the hand or shoulder. This piece, although it was known as a "light field gun," certainly qualifies. The weapon was one of the first to incorporate a hydropneumatic recoil system, which allowed it to remain relatively stationary after firing. The "trail" (where the dog is sleeping) contains a spade at the end. This would dig into the ground to help keep the weapon in place during recoil. The barrel could be adjusted to shoot at angles up to nineteen degrees above the horizontal, useful in attacking an enemy hidden behind a ridge. A caisson, one of the specialized carts made famous in song, is on the left. It was used to haul the heavy three-inch shells.

68. Canteen barroom, 1895 (print 13.10). Located in Waters Hall, the canteen served light wine and beer by the glass during its existence from 1890 to 1901. Waters Hall was originally the sutler's store, long owned privately by Moses Waters. He sold the building to the government in 1889. The canteen was renamed the post exchange in 1897 (Pride, *History of Fort Riley*, pp. 198, 207, 223).

67 (opposite). George Young and friends, 1901 (print 730). As the pins on their hats indicate, these three soldiers served in Troop D of the Eighth Cavalry. They pose with rifles and sabers, but the photograph is dominated by the youthfulness of their faces.

69. Pig roast, 1905 (print 1561). These happy soldiers, posturing as though for a beer commercial, were from Troop D of the Eighth Cavalry. Their party site is unknown, but the terrain, large logs, and blanket-swathed man suggest that they were near the Republican or Kansas River.

young women. Prostitutes were easy to find, but many of the younger soldiers sought instead the company of local schoolgirls. Marshal Cullinan and his successors had a delicate job in deciding when such meetings were innocent and when they were not. Activity peaked on warm summer nights, and in August 1901, the marshal clearly thought a line had been crossed. He went on the "war path," according to a reporter, and informed townspeople that more of their daughters than ever before were "on the streets at most any time of night . . . when they should be at home." The schoolyard at Fifteenth and Washington was the prime meeting place.[99]

Being an officer in the army during the Pennell years was at least as much a social designation as a military one. All officers considered themselves privileged individuals, and those in the cavalry especially so. When this self-perception was combined with a fairly slow pace of life, such as characterized the military establishment before World War I, the result was a whirl of social activities. Hunting, trail riding, horse racing, and polo filled many leisure hours for the men. Family events were numerous as well, including parties and dinners of all sorts (fig. 70). The post commandant hosted a formal reception and dance upon the arrival of new units. Similar receptions welcomed each visiting dignitary. This, though, was just the beginning. As Margaret Clark Conless, who grew up on the post while her father served as head of the quartermaster department, remembered:

> There was always a Saturday evening "hop" with an orchestra from the regimental band playing for the dancers. . . . About once a year there was a fancy dress (costume) ball with the officers and ladies wearing beautiful costumes and wigs or with their hair powdered white. Always there was a grand march with the commanding officer and his lady leading.[100]

Partly because the corps of officers at Fort Riley was small, partly because many Junction City civic leaders were former officers, and partly because both groups were isolated, it was natural that the two communities would interact on many social occasions. The officers provided minstrels and an orchestra for a benefit to raise money for the town's poor during the Christmas season of 1895, for example. Half of the 400 couples at an exceptionally large ball hosted by the Sixth Cavalry in 1900 drove over from Junction City. And in 1903, the post sponsored a big Fourth of July celebration for the town during which 2,000 people attended the featured horse-racing event. This entertainment relationship was by no means one way. Townspeople raised several hundred dollars in 1898 for a reception to honor the troops as they returned from the war in Cuba. They hosted many private events as well, especially when a military friend was to be transferred (fig. 71).[101]

The closeness of the connection between army officers and local residents was not universal. Pennell's son, Joseph Stanley, wrote that the officers had "a faintly patronizing air" toward his father and presumably toward other merchants as well, "in the same way that an Oxford blood might speak to his unpaid tailor." Nobody enjoys being looked down upon, of course, and the younger Pennell wrote that his mother and others felt "a great bitterness" toward the group.[102] The other side of the coin came when a Fort Riley officer went on to achieve great military or other glory. Then, almost all Junction City residents were quick to embrace the man as "one of ours" and to hope that his influence might lead to increased appropriations for the old home post and town (figs. 72 and 73).

70. Party for noncommissioned officers, 1901 (print 802). NCOs occupy the slippery social ground between enlisted men and regular officers. As one means of coping, they tended to dress especially formally at their dinners. Fort Riley is the site of the earliest on-post housing ever provided for married NCOs. Significantly, it was isolated from the quarters for regular officers and constructed of brick instead of stone (see map 4).

71. Farewell banquet for Captain Claude B. Sweezy, 1905 (print 1557). To honor Captain Sweezy, who had just been assigned to Omaha to serve as paymaster, four of his Junction City friends hosted a party in the main dining room of the Bartell House. The group, which included thirteen townspeople and twenty-five officers, convened at 9:45 and stayed until after midnight. The captain was reportedly "one of the best liked men in the post" (*Junction City Union,* October 13, 1905). His hosts were Dr. Fred O'Donnell, Dr. George Spencer, realtor James Grant, and William Sweezey, the superintendent of the electric utility company.

73. Colonel Adna R. Chaffee, 1898 (print 247). Chaffee (1842–1914) married Annie F. Rockwell, the sister of local merchants Bertrand and George, on March 30, 1875. This union, which symbolized the close relations between the fort and the town, took on added significance as he quickly rose to the rank of general. He distinguished himself in Cuba in 1898 and in China during the Boxer Rebellion. Then, after serving as governor of the Philippines, he was named the army's first chief of staff. In this latter capacity he arranged for important military training maneuvers to be held at Fort Riley (*Junction City Union,* November 5, 1914).

72 (opposite). Lieutenant George C. Patton and daughter, 1914 (print 2759). Although his fame as a general during World War II came in an armored division, George Patton was a cavalryman at heart. He came to Fort Riley in 1913 to serve as Master of the Sword. Upon leaving the next year, he presented a cup to be awarded annually to the student winner of a saber competition.

Around the Town

The prosperity that Fort Riley and the Union Pacific Railroad brought to Junction City affected far more than just the appearance of the business district. When banker Sumner W. Pierce built a large new home for himself in 1895, it prompted reflection by the editor of the *Union* on housing in general. "Junction City," he wrote, "though one of the oldest and by far the most prosperous towns in all of Central Kansas, has never run to big homes and big mortgages. While this has greatly retarded the growth of the residential portion of the city, it has . . . only deferred the work until such times as the financial status of the situation would permit."[103] Because the flow of government dollars into merchant coffers was substantial and continuous by the late 1890s, this "financial status" was soon achieved.

As a wave of new housing construction spread across the city, it brought with it increased public awareness of social class, house type, and sense of neighborhood identity. These things rarely were discussed openly, of course, because they flew in the face of homilies about equality and democracy. Still, they existed and even grew stronger as some people increased their wealth and others did not. A series of maps and photographs can reconstruct part of the pattern as it had emerged by about 1910.

African Americans stood farthest outside the mainstream of Junction City life, as they did almost everywhere in the United States. Their numbers totaled 389 in the 1910 census (about 7 percent of the city's population), but prejudice denied them access to all but menial jobs or positions as hotel porters (see table 2). As a consequence, they could not afford to be selective in their housing. The distribution resembles a doughnut (map 5). Some people lived southeast and directly west of the business district, near the homes of the white families they worked for as servants. More found shelter north of Ninth Street, either near the railroad tracks or in the small houses of Cuddy's Addition in the isolated, far northwest section of town.[104]

Railroad workers constituted a second group of people perceived as culturally distinctive. A directory identified 4 of the over 200 local employees of the Union Pacific or the MKT as African American, but with the exception of the two head agents and a few others at the depots, railroaders were generally seen as blue-collar, poorly educated white men whose roots were not set firmly in Geary County soil.[105] A strong clustering of their homes near the yards and shops was predictable, and this isolation from the rest of the community allowed the stereotyping to continue unchallenged (map 6). The Pacific House (later the Savoy Hotel) at 1005–1007 North Washington served as the residential nucleus for the single men in the group.

The houses found in African American, railroad worker, and other neighborhoods of modest means fell into two general types. Older dwellings were urban variations of the popular I-house that dominated in the midwestern countryside. To fit on the narrow lots of cities, people simply rotated the traditional design ninety degrees (compare figs. 42 and 74). Sometimes they would build small one-story versions, sometimes standard two-story, four-room

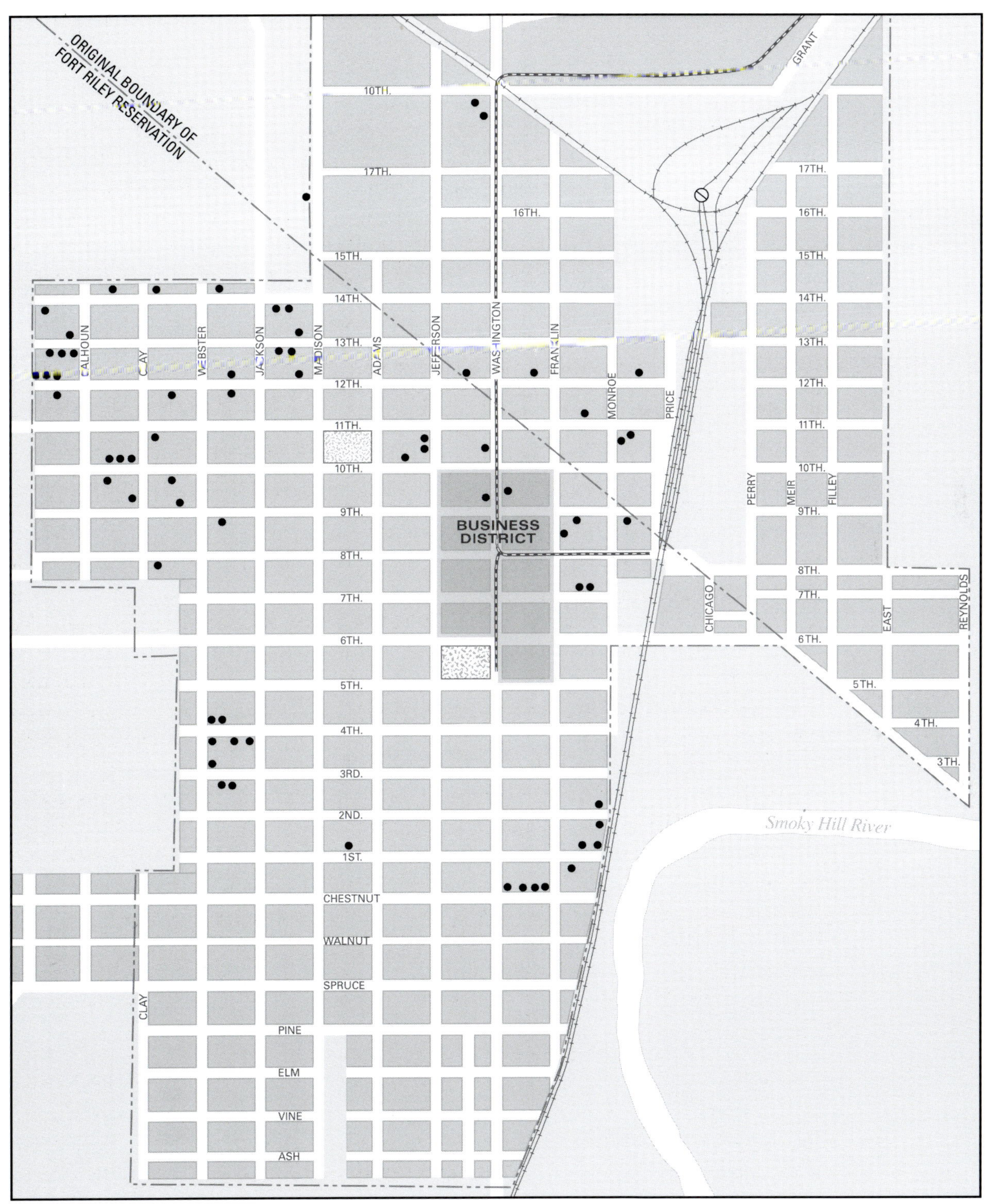

Map 5. African American Households, 1908–1909

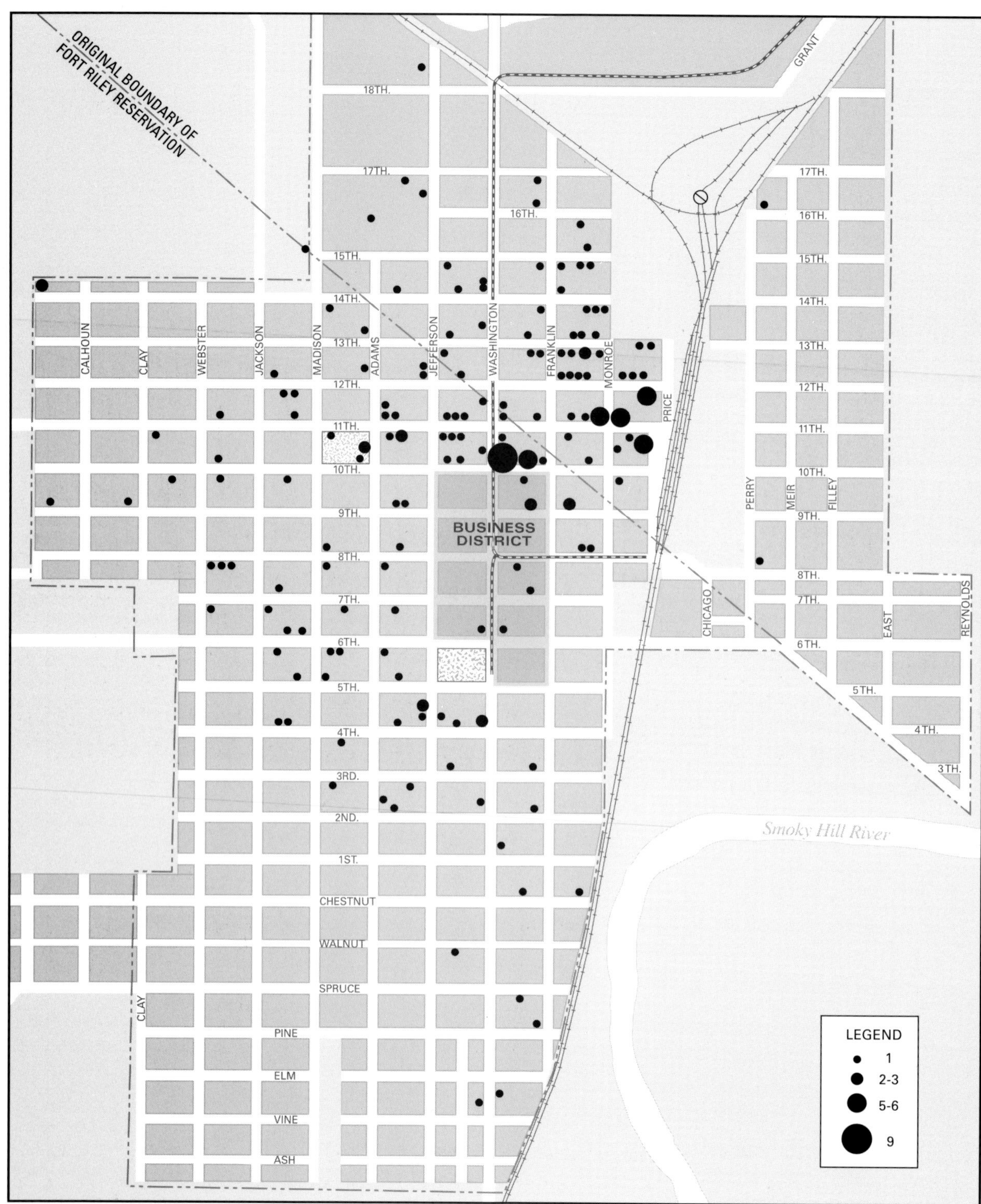

Map 6. Railroad Employees, 1908–1909

74. Charles Wisler's house, 1900 (print 569). Guttering, an accessory taken for granted by current Americans, was rare in 1900, except when rainwater was needed to fill a cistern. Residential streets were almost all dirt roads and therefore either rutted (as here) or dusty. A hitching post stands behind the buggy.

models. A third possibility, known as a one and a half, is shown in the photograph of the Charles Wisler home. Additions to the rear were almost always for a kitchen and a porch.

Next door to the Wisler home stood an example of the second house type common in working-class neighborhoods. Usually called a foursquare because of its shape (but sometimes a pyramid cottage because of its roof), this design first became popular around 1900 and was widely built into the 1920s. Junction City had them by the dozens (fig. 75). Foursquare houses were no bigger inside than most I-designs. Their popularity stemmed instead from compactness. A centrally located stove or new ductless furnace could heat four rooms fairly efficiently if they were arranged in a square. Elongated I-houses, in contrast, had been created for the now-vanishing age of multiple fireplaces.

Junction City's merchant community, always set apart from others in the city by their leadership function, became even more distinctive as they accumulated wealth in the late 1890s and early 1900s. A convenient way to identify the core group—membership in the local country club—shows a heavy concentration just south and west of the city park (map 7). The houses built in this neighborhood during the Pennell years seem at first to vary considerably. This is what might be expected from people who wanted to impress one another with their taste and financial wherewithal. They valued social acceptance at least as much as individuality, however, and upon further inspection, a family resemblance in the architecture becomes clear. Historians call it picturesque eclecticism, a selective borrowing of past European styles and adornment.

Joseph Pennell himself lived in this neighborhood. His home, which still stands at 228 West Fourth, was built in 1901. It is a variation of the simple foursquare structure (compare figs. 75 and 76). He added cross gables on the front and a two-story bay window on the parlor side to soften the form and fish-scale shingles for accent, but the basic cubic form is obvious. A person with additional money could tack on even more architectural trim. A successful cattleman, David Hill, had built what is often referred to as a Queen Anne house less than a block from the Pennell site in 1893 (fig. 77). This style, too, was frequently a marriage of an older form—in this case, an I-house—with current architectural fashion. Queen Anne designs are known for complex trimwork and roof lines. In this example, a tower clearly is the intended focal point.

A few truly wealthy businessmen (and some who wanted to appear so) built mansions during the golden age. Stephen Boon, for example, who owned a butcher shop on Washington Street but made most of his money as a meat contractor for the post, constructed a three-story, native-stone home in the southwestern corner of the city.[106] He placed emphasis on a fashionable mansard roof, an imitation of what was known as French Empire architecture (fig. 78). Contractor Walter Ziegler, in contrast, elected to reach even further back in time for inspiration and erected the closest thing to a Greek temple in town (fig. 79).

Map 7. Members of the Junction City Country Club, 1904–1911

75. John Weiss's house, 1900 (print 595.1) Young trees suggest that the Weisses' foursquare house may not be much older than the guests at their party. This house type also came in a two-story version that was popular in upper-class neighborhoods and on prosperous farms. The parapet around the chimney is not particularly common; neither is the bay window on the left. The Weiss family must have been short-time residents of the city, because they do not appear in either the 1900 census or the 1905 city directory.

76. Joseph Pennell's house, 1902 (print 856). The nearer house belonged to Pennell, but he built the farther one as well. His wife's parents, the Stanleys, lived there. The big house originally contained three bedrooms and a bath upstairs. Downstairs, a large front hall separated a double parlor on the near side from a bedroom and dining room on the west. The kitchen projects to the rear (*Junction City Union,* November 21, 1901). A portion of Centennial Hall can be glimpsed in the right background. Named for the year of its construction (1876), this building served as home to the local Universalist church at the time of the photograph.

77. William F. and Harvey A. Muenzenmayer's house, 1919 (print 3063). When constructed in 1893 by David Hill at a cost of $6,000, a reporter called this "by far the most attractive home in the city" (*Junction City Union,* October 14, 1893). It featured electric lights, hot and cold running water, and a conservatory for plants. Lumberman George T. Brown owned it early in the century, and then the Muenzenmayers. The house was converted to apartments in 1924 but restored in the 1960s; it still stands at 240 West Third (*Junction City Union,* September 12, 1993).

78. Stephen Boon's house, 1904 (print 1273). It is difficult to soften the appearance of a square limestone structure, but that was the intent of the rounded dormers and the curved, mansard roof line. Builders added intricate matching grillwork at the roof peak and over the porch for the same purpose. Indicators that the Boons' location at 106 North Jackson was remote include space for sweet corn (left back) and a road used so infrequently that grass has taken root. Note the pair of hitching posts cast in the form of tree stumps.

79. Walter Ziegler's home, 1909 (print 2150). Walter, a son of John Charles Ziegler, worked for the construction business owned by his father and uncle. Later, Walter and his brother Samuel formed their own company. The family firm built this house, which was still under construction at the time of the photograph, at 415 Walnut. It is now part of the Junction City Good Samaritan Center.

Civic Values

When the current generation of Americans views such photographs as the Boon family in front of their house (see fig. 78) or the people attending the Weiss baby party (see fig. 75), they see an array of starched collars, long skirts, and high necklines that reinforces a popular image of the early 1900s. That was a time, it would seem, of high moral values, propriety, and even primness. It is easy to find evidence to support this view. Besides dress, the national movement to ban alcohol comes quickly to mind. In Junction City and elsewhere, these years also saw the construction of one fine stone church building after another (fig. 80).

The true value system of that time was more complicated than any easy Victorian stereotype. We need to remember that people almost always put on their best and most formal clothes for a photographer, and that fewer than half of the nation's population belonged to a church. Moreover, we know that saloons operated openly in Junction City and other Kansas cities, and bootleggers flourished wherever legal outlets were quashed. Actually, instead of representing polar opposites of behavior, churches and saloons had much in common. Both offered escape and refuge for people in need.[107]

If a single overriding cultural value had to be assigned to the people of Junction City during the Pennell years, I would vote for pragmatic. Residents believed in their power to create change for the good and were guided in this pursuit by a businessman's sense of practicality and compromise. The decision to regulate saloons was made in this light. So was the subsequent one not to contest the state edict for their closure. Other examples are apparent from a study of Pennell's photographs, especially those of major civic buildings.

Consider first the town's opera house. Old accounts of Junction City contain elaborate descriptions of this grand building, which has stood at the corner of Seventh and Jefferson since 1881. So great was its importance, in fact, that when the original structure was destroyed by fire on January 20, 1898, it was rebuilt almost immediately and in near replicate fashion (figs. 81 and 82). Town realism begins with the name assigned to the facility. Everyone knew that it would be used primarily as a vaudeville theater, not as a stage for the performance of actual opera. *Theater,* however, was a word that frightened ministers and other sanctimonious citizens, because professional actors had a reputation for scandalous behavior. To gain access to the popular entertainment that most people craved (and yet not alienate an important minority group), town leaders here and elsewhere across the country solemnly stated that their primary goal was education and high culture. *Opera house* (or occasionally *lyceum*) was a label that reinforced this noble sentiment, so opera houses they became.[108]

Junction City people even took opera-house pragmatism one step further. They designed their building for multiple purposes. Quarters for the fire and police departments faced Seventh Street, with rooms above for the city council, town band, and board of education. To attend an event at the opera house proper, a person entered from the Jefferson Street side. There a carriage porch and a change from brick to stone construction signified an activity of higher cultural status.[109]

80. Universalist church, 1909 (print 2168.1). Universalists, an early split from the Congregational Church in New England, hold liberal Protestant beliefs. The denomination is rare in Kansas but flourished in early Junction City primarily because of the financial backing of three prominent men: realtor Alfred C. Pierce (from Otsego County, New York), banker Sumner Pierce (Alfred's brother), and bookseller Charles H. Trott (from Boston). The Pennells were members as well. This building at the corner of Fifth and Adams was constructed in 1908 and 1909 at a cost of $11,695 (*Junction City Union,* July 31, 1908).

81. Opera house, 1899 (print 468.12). A reconstructed opera house opened in late October 1898, only nine months after the original structure had burned. Ziegler and Dalton did the work under the direction of Topeka architect James C. Holland for a cost of about $25,000. The auditorium, with walls painted terra-cotta and gold, contained 410 seats in its lower level and 240 more in a balcony and gallery. In addition, six luxury boxes were "richly adorned with expensive silk and wool drapery" and provided with "artistic willow chairs" (*Junction City Union,* October 31, 1898).

82. Opera house stage, 1904 (print 1367). Performers at the new opera house were indulged with ten separate dressing rooms. The stage measured thirty-six feet by sixty-two feet, was raised forty-eight inches above the orchestra pit, and was lit by 250 lights arranged on thirty different circuits (*Junction City Union,* October 31, 1898). Thomas W. Dorn, the longtime manager, arranged for a wide variety of entertainment. Regular local performers included the Junction City Dramatic Club, high school lecturers, and ladies' groups from the Episcopal, Methodist, and Universalist churches. The opening production, however, was a rendition of a comic opera, *The White Milk Flag,* by a "strong New York company of thirty-five people" (*Junction City Union,* June 24, 1898). To ensure a steady stream of such players, Dorn joined the Kansas Theatrical Association, a group that maintained a booking agent in Chicago (*Junction City Union,* September 28, 1895).

Visitors to the city in the 1880s often commented on the attractive clock tower that topped the original opera house and were impressed with the cultural aspirations the building represented. They were surprised, however, not to see a similar tower attached to a grand courthouse. Junction City residents were very much aware of this absence themselves. Indeed, they regarded it as a flaw and began to make serious plans for a new courthouse building in the late 1890s. Money was not a problem. A referendum that authorized $35,000 in bonds passed easily, thereby ensuring that both the practical and the symbolic needs of the community could be met. Location, though, was a matter for debate. The existing small courthouse on Eighth Street, between Washington and Franklin, sat in a bad neighborhood. In fact, it was "chucked up face to face with a dozen out houses, little shanties and a sporting house almost large enough to overshadow" any new structure.[110]

County commissioners mulled over four possible sites in the spring of 1899: the old location, property owned by Thomas Dixon on Washington Street near Sixth, lots on Seventh Street between Washington and Franklin, and the city park. They eliminated the park because of questions over its legal title, but all the other new places had their champions. Still, the old site won out. The reasoning, as succinctly expressed by the town sage, Bertrand Rockwell, was pure pragmatism. The environs on Eighth Street could easily be improved, he said, and that place "is about the dividing line in population of our city." Just a year later, a stately Romanesque building constructed of the best local limestone was ready for occupation (figs. 83 and 84).[111]

One of the problems that accompanies prosperity is increased expectations. Few people objected to the priority given to the opera house and the courthouse, but what civic buildings should come next? Three major contenders arose. Many people saw a need for a new high school to replace a cramped building. Other groups lobbied for two new public structures: a free library and a hospital. Newspapermen, always boosters, saw merit in each proposal, but most citizens seemed to feel that doctors could finance their own medical facility. Women from the elite Ladies' Reading Club gathered signatures to put the library issue on the ballot for April 1903, where it would join a bond proposal for a high school that been placed there without any special backing.[112]

Sensing the potential for divisiveness, *Union* reporters published the results of the election without comment. Voters approved $30,000 for the high school by a three-to-one margin (fig. 85). Several hundred fewer people cast ballots on the library issue, and those who did rejected it by a slim margin of ten votes. Elitism likely was the deciding factor here, perhaps working in two ways. Ordinary citizens saw a library as a luxury compared with a school. If the Junction City experience was anything like that described for Xenia, Ohio, some of the more prudish citizens likely preferred the library system as it was—a private one managed by the Ladies' Reading Club. With this arrangement, a person could be assured that all the books available would be wholesome and that only people who washed their hands regularly would read them. That the women owned their own club building to house this library may have been a factor as well (fig. 86).[113]

84. Courtroom, 1900 (print 595.11). If the stage of the opera house symbolized local cultural aspirations, then the courtroom certainly did the same for democratic ideals. This photograph focuses on the bar, a partition that separates the court proper from the gallery. The woman likely was the plaintiff in this case, her attorney the person addressing the jury. Juries stayed all male in Geary County until November 1919 (*Junction City Union,* October 16, 1919). Note the transom windows and high ceiling, which provided relief from the intense summer heat in this second-story room. The presence of electric fixtures without exposed wiring was a rarity in 1900.

83 (opposite). Courthouse, 1899 (print 595.6). Although public funds underwrote this building, it was H. H. ("Hass") Ziegler's gift to the city in many ways. Ziegler, a partner in the town's preeminent construction company, served on the county commission. He rallied support for the project, drew up the specifications, and then politely resigned just before the call for bids. The *Union* editor estimated that Hass's knowledge and volunteer work saved the county $2,500 (June 2, 1899). The courthouse area was one of the first in the city to have concrete sidewalks instead of limestone slabbing.

85. Junction City High School, 1904 (print 1221). The Junction City Board of Education selected Topeka architect James C. Holland to design the new building, the same man who had overseen the opera house and the courthouse. His exterior, a Romanesque plan that emphasizes an off-center, arched main entrance, echoes the courthouse in several ways. Ziegler and Dalton did the actual construction and installed, among other features, "the best quarter-sawed yellow pine flooring." The board voted down a move to name the building after President Roosevelt, who had visited town in 1903 (*Junction City Union,* September 11, 1903; March 4, 1904). Workers were not quite finished with all the details when Pennell took this photograph.

86. Ladies' Reading Club building, 1912 (print 2584.20). A group of businessmen's wives, who had met originally in 1874 to solicit aid for victims of a statewide plague of grasshoppers, decided to organize permanently the next spring as a social and study club. They were the second group in the state to do so. Clubwomen were overwhelmed in 1897 when Bertrand Rockwell built a graceful cottage at 224 North Jefferson as a gift to the organization. The structure has two main rooms—an auditorium and a library—and came equipped with hard pine woodwork, brass knobs and hinges, and a baby grand piano. At the dedication, Rockwell praised the serious nature of the study he had witnessed and termed it "a postgraduate course at home" (*Junction City Union,* September 3, 1897).

The library issue faded from public discourse for two years after the 1903 election. Then, suddenly, it was resolved overnight. A reclusive businessman, George Smith, willed two commercial lots at the southwest corner of Seventh and Washington to the city, plus his estate of $22,500. All was for the construction and maintenance of a library. This money was sufficient to create a first-class facility, and Smith's practicality ensured that the legacy would be enduring. The library was to be located on the second floor of a new building to be erected on his downtown lots (figs. 87 and 88). The ground and basement levels were to be rented out to businesses; this would generate funds to purchase books and pay the librarians' salaries. Smith's executors estimated that the initial rents would be $4,320 per year, and the amounts remained sufficient to fund the library entirely until 1944.[114]

In addition to an array of impressive buildings, Junction City people erected two major public monuments during their golden age. This pair reveals values beyond pragmatism. The first of the two, an arch erected in 1898 to honor the Grand Army of the Republic (GAR), was a tribute to the Civil War veterans who had settled the city and were now nearly gone. It was an openly sentimental gesture, and also a self-congratulatory one. Pioneer hardships, it implied, had been replaced by prosperity and progressive ideas, but the people had not forgotten their heritage. As an additional sign of their sincerity, citizens selected the most prominent site in town for their tribute—the northeast corner of the city park, directly across from the Bartell House (fig. 89).[115]

Motives behind the second monument were more complex, but self-promotion certainly was one factor. In 1902, a group assembled to dedicate an obelisk in honor of an Indian settlement called Quivira. This was the famous, supposedly wealthy site that had been the objective of the Coronado expedition north from Mexico in 1541. No one knew its exact location, but a local man, Robert Henderson, had convinced himself that Junction City was the place. When his beliefs were reinforced by the findings of archaeologist Jacob Brower, he decided to build a monument. Most local people were not so sure about the claim, but everybody recognized that any publicity surrounding it would help the city. Thus, the unveiling ceremony at Logan's Grove on the Henderson farm just south of town was well attended (fig. 90).[116]

Personal Values

That the cultural messages conveyed by public memorials might differ from those of civic buildings should not be surprising. Human beings are complicated creatures, after all, and any attempt to describe a community's value system is prone to oversimplification. The best remedy, perhaps, is to sample from as many perspectives as possible. Pennell allows us considerable flexibility and range in doing this for Junction City. He supplemented his standard studio portraits and studies of new buildings with several trips inside people's homes. He also was present at weddings and funerals, and at sporting events and parties. He even photographed advertising displays in store windows. If we look at these things carefully, they can reveal much about everyday tastes, beliefs, and behaviors.

87. George Smith Library, 1908 (print 1998). This photograph, taken from almost the same spot as figure 17, reveals a profound transformation of Junction City's most important business intersection. James C. Holland was again chosen as the architect, but he selected a Greek Revival style instead of the Romanesque he had used on the high school and courthouse. The building is ninety feet long and forty-eight feet deep, with Corinthian columns of red granite providing an accent for the main limestone body. Five business locations were envisioned on the main floor, but only a milliner had moved in at the time of the photograph. The railing to the right of the three men shields a stairwell to the basement level (*Junction City Union,* February 2, 1906; May 25, 1906).

88. Interior of the George Smith Library, 1908 (print 1997). Ziegler and Dalton brought their usual concern for quality to the Smith project. The library level had an eighteen-foot ceiling and was well lit with windows at two elevations. With expansion in mind, it provided space for 18,000 books, even though the collection numbered only 4,000 at the opening in March 1908. The weight of the books was borne by a series of large iron pillars, each covered with oak paneling. Inspection of the photograph reveals steam heat, expensive lighting fixtures, a newspaper rack, and an umbrella stand. The stairs on the left are the main entrance up from the street level. They face the circulation counter (*Junction City Union,* February 2, 1906; August 17, 1906; December 1, 1985; May 4, 1997).

89. GAR monument, 1898 (print 260). To honor veterans of the Grand Army of the Republic, the Junction City community raised $1,800 for a dignified arch. Some of the money came from schoolchildren who sold commemorative buttons for fifty cents apiece. The archway itself is eight feet wide and sixteen feet tall, with the entire structure spanning twenty-three feet at the base and reaching thirty-five feet into the air ("nearly as high" as the Bartell House). The architect was F. A. Gardner from Fort Riley, and the contractor Ziegler and Dalton. Six thousand people braved a September rain to attend the dedication in 1898 (*Junction City Union,* November 5, 1897; September 18, 1898).

90. Quivira monument, 1902 (print 911). Robert Henderson, a Union veteran, believed so strongly that Quivira, the wealthy Indian city sought by Coronado, lay near Junction City that he financed this monument himself. When his granddaughter, Helen Ritter, pulled the cord, people saw a granite obelisk seventeen and a half feet tall. The unveiling, which took place August 15, 1902, included a salute by the Sixth Battery field artillery (*Junction City Union,* August 15, 1902).

Home interiors, perhaps the most traditional repository of personal values, are an obvious place to begin. No one would have considered taking a formal photograph of a bedroom or kitchen, but several views exist of parlors, sitting rooms, and other semipublic locations. The furnishings of the Frank Otis family and of Mary Ann Wetzel, for example, display some differences in taste because of the ages of their occupants, but also many commonalities (figs. 91 and 92). A show window from a local furniture store provides additional insights (fig. 93).

Dark colors dominate in these settings—the woodwork, the furniture, and the rugs. Although taste does not necessarily require a rational explanation, these somber tones almost certainly relate to the difficulties even a fastidious homemaker had in keeping dirt (and usually tobacco spittle, too) at bay. No one had an electric sweeper, of course, and windows had to be kept open in the summer. Clouds of dust thus poured in from unpaved roads. Winter, with its soot from coal or wood fires, was no better. Even the ubiquitous coal-oil lamps smoked on occasion.

A self-conscious attempt of people to align themselves with nature is a second theme linking these three rooms. Many writers have interpreted the intricacies of Queen Anne architecture as part of a concern with "organic complexity" (see fig. 77), but the concept is much more developed in interior furnishings. Look, for example, at the floral wallpaper in Mary Ann Wetzel's room and in Dumm's store display. Similar designs mark all the carpets, some of the wall hangings, and, of course, the Otis's pastoral painting. Naturalistic wicker, Mrs. Otis's choice as a chair material, gives a more tangible expression to this concern. So does the fan palm in the store window. Even the popularity of rocking chairs fits with the general orientation.

To modern eyes, the interiors of a century ago also bring to mind the adjectives ornate and cluttered. People in 1904 or so placed a much different judgment on this appearance, of course. They called it picturesque and worked diligently to attain a complex mosaic of styles and textures. Part of the effect comes from attempts to evoke nature, such as the feather in Mrs. Wetzel's vase, but most authorities interpret such rooms as a demonstration of America's coming of age. People were shedding the austere existence of pioneers and becoming familiar with the artistic traditions of the European past. Moreover, their confidence was such that they actively created new forms within this heritage rather than merely copying it. They mixed and matched the ancient Mediterranean with the High Gothic and unself-consciously engraved acanthus leaves onto the sides of their new electrical fixtures.

Pianos and organs, centerpieces of most middle-class homes of the time, epitomized the creative mixture of purpose and design. These instruments stood first as symbols for the fine arts, the sophisticated aspirations of a family. By enabling group singing, they also acted to bond people together. An organ would supply additional religious and moral connotations. Finally, as demonstrated by Mary Ann Wetzel, these instruments provided another way to express picturesque design in furniture, as well as a nice display area for bowls, photographs, and vases.

Product exhibits that merchants assembled for their windows provide another good vehicle for studying personal taste. New products were coming on the market rapidly at this

91. Lieutenant Frank Otis and family, 1903 (print 1144). Lieutenant Otis was much more family- and community-minded than most army officers. A *Union* reporter called him "better known in this city than any other person in the post," and he resigned from the service in 1905 rather than be transferred to the Philippines and leave his wife and children (July 21, 1905). Sailor outfits, such as those worn by the three boys, were popular at the time. Mrs. Otis is reading with her son about boxing.

92. Mary Ann Wetzel's room, 1901 (print 725). Mrs. Wetzel was eighty-one years old at the time of this photograph. She had been confined to a wheelchair since 1886 and widowed since 1889. The single curtain over her window suggests poverty, but she overcame her problems by being a faithful, Bible-reading member of the Methodist Episcopal church (*Junction City Union,* December 25, 1903).

93. Dumm's window, 1901 (print 633). William C. Dumm had just come to Junction City in 1901 but would soon expand his business into a second storefront on Washington Street. He carried a wide range of goods, including rocking chairs from $3.50 to $37.50 and iron beds from $2.35 to $35.00. Velour couches sold for $6.00, tapestry ones for $7.50, and leather ones for $27.50 (*Junction City Union,* September 27, 1901). This photograph is dominated by portieres, hangings made from netted cords of silk, cotton, or, occasionally, beads and bamboo. They were advertised as a way to soften hard lines and to add a touch of color.

time, people had the money to buy, and store owners had begun to realize that an elaborate show window was an effective means of advertising. Some of these displays were true works of art, and we are fortunate that their creators occasionally were proud enough to call in a photographer.

Several of Pennell's most intriguing compositions feature patent medicines (fig. 94). These bottles and boxes, often bearing pictures of distinguished-looking men or nurturing grandmothers, promised to cure almost anything that ailed you. Advertisements, mostly in the form of personal testimonials, covered a fair percentage of every issue of the *Union* and almost every other newspaper of the time. If these claims seem foolish to us today, it is only because medical knowledge has advanced astonishingly far between 1900 and 2000. Doctors in the Pennell years were caring people by and large, but they could do little more than set bones, wait for fevers to take their course, and administer alcohol or laudanum if the pain was severe. In desperation, people would listen to messages of hope from "Dr. Pierce" or almost anybody else.

Grocery store displays would seem to be far removed from the world of patent medicines, but the link between health and diet was as exploited a century ago as it is now. The C. W. Post Company was one of the leaders (fig. 95). Postum, for example, a substitute for coffee, was marketed partly on its own merits and partly with claims that the consumption of regular coffee and caffeine might lead to loss of eyesight. Grape-Nuts cereal was developed in 1898 as another coffee substitute. Its conversion to a cereal ("fully cooked, pre-digested") came only after sales lagged. The claim for Grape-Nuts as a brain food, as shown in the photograph, was based on an ingredient called "natural phosphate of potash."[117]

Brand-name goods, as represented by Pierce's medicines and Post's Grape-Nuts, were not unknown in the nineteenth century, but their big push to dominance came early in the 1900s. As part of this, manufacturers of such products provided many of the signs and advertising copy used in the show windows. Junction City stores participated in National Canned-Foods Week in 1913, for example, during which banners heralded the advantages of "sterilized food in a sterilized can" and made the odd claim that "canned foods are fresh foods," because only a few hours elapsed between the field and the factory. Two years later, ninety-five companies united for an even broader campaign—Nationally Advertised Goods Week (fig. 96).[118] Besides growing steadily more elaborate over the years, store-window displays also moved into new areas of marketing. By the 1910s, Junction City customers could occasionally pocket a free gift with some of their purchases (fig. 97). They also could inspect bedclothes and even the undergarments of men and women alike (fig. 98). Once started, advertising seemed to recognize no limits.

An observer of Junction City life at the turn of the century need not have relied only on the indirect measures of room furnishings or advertising displays. Without the television sets and long commutes to work that tend to isolate modern Americans, people during these years always seemed to be attending some event or joining a new club or volunteer group. With Pennell's assistance, we can sample much of this.

94. Display of Dr. Pierce's medicines, 1904 (print 1198.1). Someone at Loeb and Hollis's drugstore created this elaborate window arrangement, complete with peace lilies, parlor palms, and a portrait of R. V. Pierce of Buffalo, New York. The two products shown had overlapping clienteles, but the Favorite Prescription was aimed primarily at women. An advertisement that ran many times in the *Union* read as follows: "The fear of motherhood is rapidly passing away and nothing has done so much to drive it away as the record of Dr. Pierce's Favorite Prescription. Dr. Pierce has held that the danger and pain at the time of parturition were really unnecessary and unnatural, and that if every woman were healthy and strong as Nature meant her to be this function would be performed painlessly and safely. . . . The organs directly involved may be strengthened, purified, invigorated for the time of trial, and for this purpose Dr. Pierce's Favorite Prescription has been used with success by hundreds of thousands of women. It is the product of the skill and experience of a regularly graduated physician—a skilled specialist who for over thirty years has successfully treated the diseases of women. Unlike many modern medicines Dr. Pierce's Favorite Prescription . . . contains no whiskey, alcohol, sugar, syrup, opium, or narcotic of any kind and its use does not, therefore, create a craving for stimulants" (February 17, 1899).

95. Display of C. W. Post products, 1905 (print 1543). The big red dot ("It makes red blood"), shown here in Rockwell's window, appeared on most Post products. This and other company claims about healthful foods were attacked in 1911 by reporters for *Collier's Magazine.* Before he achieved fame as a cereal manufacturer, Post ran a hardware store in Independence, Kansas, in the 1870s. After retiring, he created the utopian community of Post in western Texas (Bruce and Crawford, *Cerealizing America,* pp. 24–32).

96. Brand-name goods display, 1915 (print 2786). Rockwell's store ran a full-page advertisement in the *Union* for Nationally Advertised Goods Week. Part of the text read as follows: "There was a day, not so long ago, when you knew little of what you bought, who made it or where it came from. Oat meal was just oat meal; cooking utensils were just pots and pans; glassware had no special identifying name; you bought simply furniture; and toilet preparations were orphans. And the buyer in the small town did not get the improved and better things that were only for the city dweller alone. But it's different now. You order by name—today you ask for Kellogg's Corn Flakes, Nesco Enameled Ware, Heisey Glassware, Berkey and Gay Furniture, Colgate's toilet preparations—you know who makes them, you know where the factory is, you know what goes into the goods and what they will do for you. Advertising tells you. The goods are guaranteed to us, and by us to you, by the country's biggest and most successful manufacturers, the makers of Nationally Advertised Goods" (March 18, 1915).

97. Nine O'clock shoes display, 1914 (print 2776). The Dittman Company, a reputable firm from Saint Louis, had been making shoes since 1845. Their children's selections, all high topped, sold from $2.00 to $2.75 (*Junction City Union,* August 27, 1914). Overwhelming the shoes, however, is an obvious appeal to patriotism. War was under way in Europe at this time. Americans, although still hoping to remain neutral, had already begun to unite around their national symbols.

98. Corset display, 1916 (print 2869.1). Advertisements for corsets can be found in local newspapers into the 1920s, but their purpose was undergoing a rapid change at the time the Crockett Dry Goods Company prepared this display of W. B. Nuform products. Before 1915, extremely tight lacing was still the fashion in the Midwest. This thrust the upper half of the body forward above a tiny waist and the lower half to the rear. The corsets pictured here were designed more to slim than to shape, and Crockett's carried newer front-laced models as well as traditional ones that cinched from the back. The prices ranged from $1 to $5 (*Junction City Union,* April 6, 1916).

Sports were as popular then as now, at least for males. Most of this activity was informal in nature, with fishing and hunting leading the way. As for team sports, high schools and universities were just beginning to get involved. In the absence of school sponsorship, community associations became the prime movers, especially for baseball. Business leaders saw the fun to be had, of course. But they also eyed possibilities for raising the level of town pride and attracting new customers to their stores.

Cities in Kansas had sponsored baseball teams as early as 1867, when Lawrence, Leavenworth, and Topeka played for the championship at the state fair. Junction City joined the action during the 1870s in a rather informal way. With the prosperity of the 1890s, however, eleven businessmen formed the Junction City Athletic Association and decided to compete at a top semiprofessional level. They raised over $800, built a ball park, advertised, and worked hard to recruit a team (figs. 99–101). The promoters saw their task as a business venture and went about it meticulously:

> As to a team, there is but one thought in the association. The very best men for the money will be employed. Every man will go in under contract, or he will not go in. There will be no bums on the team, and the first time a man is detected dissipating he will be fired bodily. We are to have a team—the men are to be ball players, and they are to be gentlemen. Wilson, the best athlete in the state, has been hired. Dunn, the gentleman who played such superb ball at second, has also been employed, and will probably be captain.[119]

All worked as planned, at least for a few years. The high point came in late May 1896, when nearly 500 local fans chartered seven coaches on a special train to Leavenworth. They went "to see Junction City's great team wipe the earth with what is said to be the best aggregation in Kansas."[120]

The same money that enabled businessmen to move baseball from cow pastures to a manicured stadium changed other sports as well. Swimming, for example, which had been a fixture for town children at the south bridge area on the Smoky Hill, was shifted into a new concrete "tank." The prime mover here was Sumner Pierce, head of the Central National Bank. Pierce believed that regular swimming would have helped him overcome a childhood infirmity, and he wanted all local children to have that advantage. A committee selected a wooded area for a park site, about a mile west of town on Fifth Street. Then, in a typically first-class procedure, they hired the state architect from Topeka, John F. Stanton, to draw up the plans (fig. 102).[121]

Along with baseball, the town band was another group activity used to promote community pride. Bands and baseball teams actually had much in common. Both were flashy, active endeavors that appealed to the American love of energy and progress. Their resplendent uniforms projected dignity and quality, and they had the ability to entertain large numbers of people. Also like baseball, bands had not yet become a common activity in schools, so town ensembles had the domain largely to themselves. Records show a band in Junction City as early as 1868, but the local movement effectively began with George Kilian. He was a barber and grocer who organized a group in 1878 and served as its leader for the next twenty-one years (fig. 103).[122]

99. Baseball diamond, 1896 (print 89.4). The Junction City Athletic Association built this beautiful field in 1895 in the block bounded by Tenth and Eleventh Streets between Adams and Madison. Members paid $50 for grading, $35 for a grandstand that seated 700 people, and $300 for an eight-foot, solid-wood fence in the outfield (*Junction City Union,* July 6, 1895; December 28, 1895). Emporia was a rival in the short-lived Kansas State and Northern Kansas Leagues. The Junction City Imperials beat them three times on this field in 1896.

100. Baseball parade, 1896 (print 69). Promoting home games was standard practice in most communities, but Junction City was lucky to find the charismatic Zeke Guddy to do so. Guddy had lived in town since retiring from the Ninth Cavalry in 1882 (*Junction City Union,* June 17, 1905). A military bugle added to his appeal.

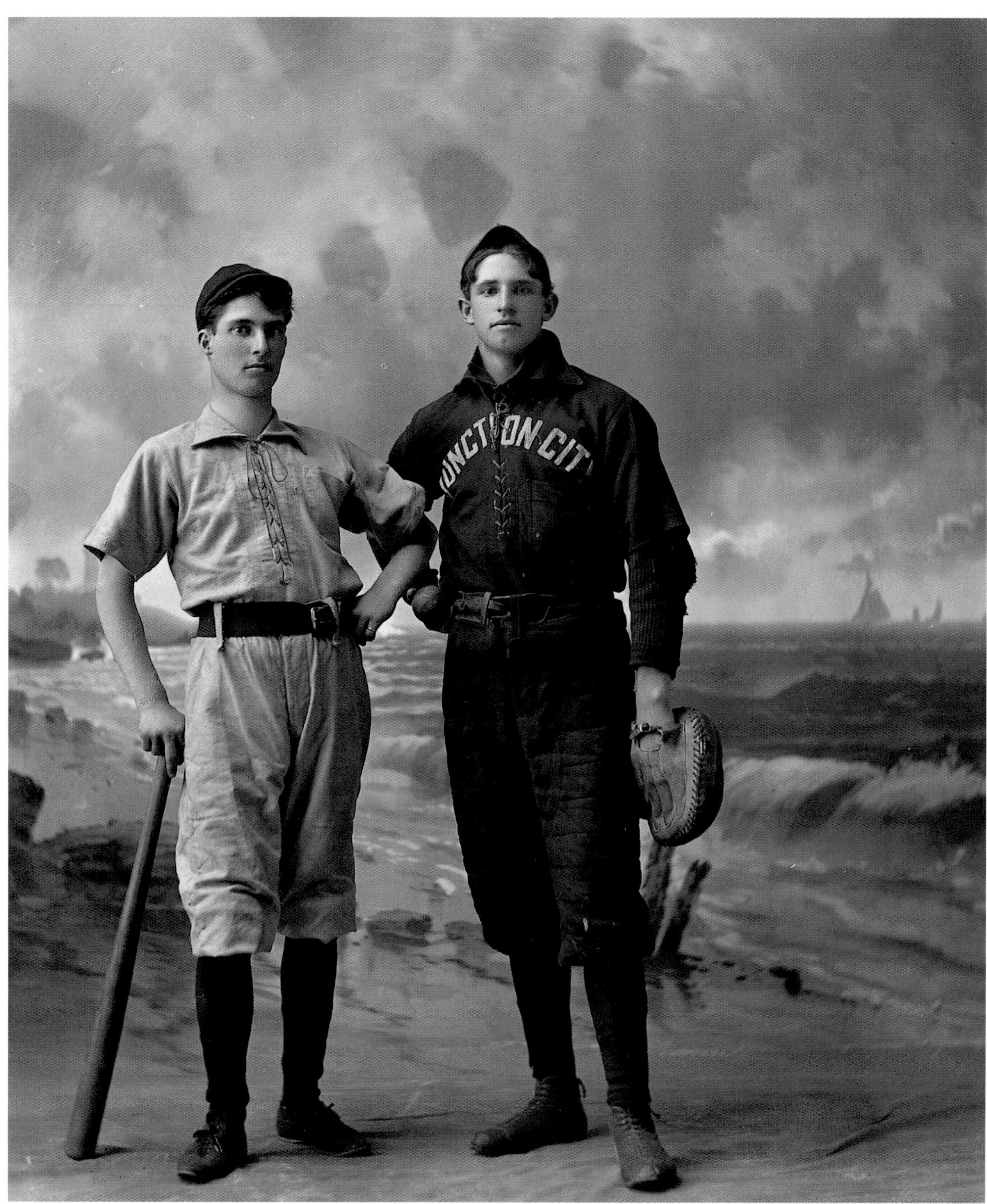
UNCTION CIT

102. Swimming pool, 1913 (print 2703.1). The Junction City pool, one of the first public swimming facilities in Kansas, measured thirty-five by seventy-five feet and cost $1,316. With accompaniments that included a wading area, a water heater, and brick dressing rooms, it was immediately popular after opening on August 19, 1913. Manager John Rogers enforced strict regulations on clothing: "Boys' and men's bathing suits shall consist of either a union suit with shirt or a two-piece bathing suit with the shirt worn outside. Girls' and ladies' bathing suits shall consist of blouse, bloomers, skirt and hose" (*Junction City Union,* August 22, 1912; September 12, 1912; June 18, 1995).

101 (opposite). Frank Barber (left) and Bert Young in baseball suits, 1899 (print 412). Looking out of place against one of Pennell's studio backdrops, these were local boys, not outside professionals. Although Young carries a catcher's mitt, both men were outfielders, with Young serving as player-manager for this season. Barber left Junction City in 1900 to be a traveling salesman for the Star Pants Company of Kansas City. Young became an engineer on the Union Pacific (*Junction City Union,* June 9, 1899; May 4, 1900; December 17, 1914).

103. Junction City band, 1898 (print 251.2). Although membership in this group was not open to women and African Americans, it did feature a wide range of ages and occupations. The band practiced three times a week in a room above Trott's bookstore and gave summer concerts in the city park. Financing came mostly from public subscriptions, with some from the city. George Kilian, the longtime leader of the group, is the sixth man from the left in the front row. He died suddenly in 1899 at the age of forty-five (*Junction City Union,* May 18, 1895; October 31, 1898; May 26, 1899; March 15, 1987).

A lack of athletic or musical ability was no barrier to participation in group activity. Social and service organizations of all types abounded; there were so many, in fact, that it seemed every citizen must belong to more than one. Some groups went by initials in their regular reports for local newspapers (A.C.E., O.N.O.), others by frivolous names (Ha Ha, High Five, Jolly Time), and still others by more serious titles (Columbian, Tribe of Ben Hur). Seemingly every national fraternal group existed as well: Eagles, Elks, Knights of Pythias (including a separate African American chapter), Masons, Odd Fellows, and Modern Woodmen of America.[123] Of these, the Masonic lodge was the largest and most prestigious (fig. 104). If a person desired action rather than talk from his or her group, that, too, was easy to find. The volunteer fire department was perhaps the most obvious choice for men (fig. 105).

Home entertainment filled in the gaps on a person's social calendar. Most of this consisted of informal gatherings to catch up on local affairs, to introduce visiting relatives to the neighborhood, or perhaps to listen to someone play the piano. Machines called phonographs or gramophones were another reason to assemble. Although expensive, their ability to bring famous singers and orchestras into one's parlor was hard to resist (fig. 106). Young women especially loved the new devices, although they would meet for almost any excuse (fig. 107).

The most elaborate of the group social activities was a pioneering venture called a country club. This idea emerged in 1901 from a group of businessmen who wanted a convenient place to hunt and fish. Lakes were not abundant in the area, but one existed six miles northeast of town, where the Kansas River had changed course sometime in the past and left a shallow, crescent-shaped lagoon at the base of a pleasant, wooded escarpment (see map 1). These men arranged a lease in 1903 and made plans to stock the water with black bass and crappie. As word spread of these preparations and people came to inspect the setting, women began to get involved. Soon Whiskey Lake was rechristened the Junction City Country Club, and about twenty-five cottages were built, along with a combination clubhouse–dancing pavilion, six boat landings, and a stable (fig. 108). It became first the most fashionable place to entertain in the summer months, and then a nearly full-time summer retreat for the fifty or so families who belonged. As one member recalled: "The principal feature of the cottages is their wide porches, which are enclosed with screen wire. There the whole family may sleep, as it were in the open air, getting all the cool breezes coming down from the Smoky Hill bluffs."[124]

Although most group activities had a social component, many were organized with education primarily in mind. Education, in fact, was unusually important during these years. Historians often label this the Progressive Era in the United States, and the term fits my reading of local events as well. Technological growth surrounded these people—everything from phonographs to tractors—and they came to believe that science and rational thought could make nearly every aspect of life better. Men began to attend seminars and read reports on new animal breeds and business management techniques. Women embraced "home economics" and listened attentively as experts told them the latest research findings on child care, public health, and education. Cooking and nutrition were especially popular subjects. More than sixty ladies signed up, for example, when "Miss Andrews, a member of the New York Cooking School," gave a seminar in February 1900 at the Universalist church (fig. 109).[125]

105. Fire wagon, 1904 (print 1334). Horse-pulled fire equipment had begun to replace manual hose carts in bigger cities as early as the 1850s. Junction City residents purchased their new wagon relatively late, in 1903, but it was a premium unit manufactured by the Seagrave Company in Columbus, Ohio. For $1,500, the city got a modern, sixty-gallon chemical tank with a 150-foot hose plus ladders, axes, lanterns, and 1,000 feet of regular water hose. The wagon's steel (not wood) body was painted white, a striking counterpoint to its crimson running gear, nickel-plated trim, and gilt lettering. For $100 more, officials also decided to purchase a "Hale patent" harness system. This was suspended above the place of each horse and, in theory, could be slipped down and attached in only three to five seconds (*Junction City Union,* June 19, 1903; November 6, 1903). Fire Chief Frank C. Trott sits next to the driver.

104 (opposite). George A. Rockwell as a Knight Templar, 1896 (print 25). An avoidance of any one religious, political, or economic creed was central to the growth of Masonic lodges in Junction City and elsewhere. So was their emphasis on raising money for health care and homes for the aged. Knight Templar is the highest degree in the York Rite of the association. The sword and multiple crosses on Rockwell's costume refer to the original Knights Templar, who protected pilgrims at Jerusalem in the twelfth century. Junction City Masons bought the large Waters hardware building in 1913 and remodeled its top two floors for their use (see figure 14). The new facility opened in 1921 (*Junction City Union,* June 26, 1913; April 14, 1921).

106. Victrola display, 1912 (print 2567). Despite selling for high prices, phonographs were popular enough by 1912 that the Durland-Sawtell Furniture Company at 117–119 West Seventh devoted nearly an entire room to them. This was a Victrola agency, a brand symbolized by a dog that recognized his master's voice on the magical machine (see the background of the photograph). Portable models (on the right) sold for between $10 and $100. The leggy cabinet version nearby (Model X) was $75; Models XI, XV, and XVI cost $100, $150, and $200, respectively (*Junction City Union,* November 28, 1912). The success of phonographs is said to have forced the motion-picture industry to move from silent films to talkies in order to compete.

107. Anna Murray party, 1912 (print 2547). Anna Murray (far left), who worked as a clerk in her parents' Homestead Bakery, decided to entertain friends during the Christmas holiday season with a Japanese chafing-dish party. It was a good occasion to don silken costumes of the thinner, looser-fitting style that was just beginning to come into fashion. Needlework also was popular with Anna's guests. Jennie Clark stands next to the hostess. Across the back row, left to right, are Marjorie Clarke, Emma McArthur, Louise Ruthert, and Carrie Clark. Seated in front are Helena Kramer (left) and Mary Clarke (*Junction City Union,* January 2, 1913). A panoramic photograph of the University of Kansas hangs on the wall.

108. Junction City Country Club, 1907 (print 1875). This view, looking northwest from the bluffs, shows the Kansas River in the background. The clubhouse, marked by a flag, was the only building wired for electricity. The newly planted trees are elms. Although members and outsiders considered the country club a model for other communities and it was featured as such in *Kansas Magazine,* the facility endured less than twenty years. Golf began to grow in popularity, and members experimented with a course at the top of the bluff. Its inconvenient site, however, led to a decision to create a completely new club on Eighth Street just west of downtown (*Junction City Union,* May 6, 1910; July 24, 1919; July 22, 1920; August 12, 1920).

109. Cooking school, 1900 (print 638.11). Miss Andrews was a ten-year veteran of cooking demonstrations when she set up shop in the basement of the Universalist church. She earned a fee, but the church received money from the sale of cooking-utensil sets she brought along. According to a report in the *Union,* the initial lesson was a success: "The Royal Diplomatic pudding was first in order, and when it came out of the mould in the shape of a watermelon with green rind and pink interior, each looker-on declared to herself that she must make one. The oyster patties were tasty, as was also the Easter salad with its tinted eggs in a nest of shredded cabbage. It is needless to say that cooking is now the chief topic of conversation among feminine minds" (February 9, 1900).

Progress and education meant more than the acceptance of sewing machines and new recipes. For many women, it was a challenge to learn about fine arts, history, and literature so that they might enrich their lives and those of their families. They also desired a forum in which they could address broader social issues such as sanitation, school standards, and aid for the poor. To these ends, study clubs became a powerful vehicle. A few, such as the Women's Christian Temperance Union, were single purpose. Most mixed literature with advocacy, however, and usually did so at every meeting. African American women were no different from their white counterparts in these goals (fig. 110).[126]

Like in all places, life in Junction City generally fell into a series of routines. Even club meetings, band practices, and most other group activities were regular and expected. Sometimes, however, an unusual or unexpected event would bring everyone together. These occasions—when rich men truly rubbed shoulders with the poor, and the young mixed with the old—tended to be long remembered. They probably also reveal small towns at their best.

From my understanding of Junction City during the golden years, true community togetherness occurred on five different occasions. We have no Pennell photograph of the armistice celebration after World War I, but he was very much on the scene for the other four. The first, an extravagant party for the Fourth of July in 1902, was self-created. The city's commercial club, which had been organized in 1900 to promote business, confidently decided to stage "the biggest celebration in Kansas" and then went out and did so. Members solicited money from merchants and set about inviting numerous bands plus "fire departments, flambeau clubs, high wire and trapeze acts, grand choruses," and more.[127]

Word of the festivities was spread with thousands of flyers, and when the weather cooperated, this day became "one of the greatest in the town's history." Excursion cars on the MKT brought in 450 people from Council Grove and beyond, four extra cars came from Clay Center and Concordia on the Fort Kearney branch, and the main Union Pacific line filled nine special cars from the east and ten from the west. When local people were counted, it was "the biggest, merriest, good-natured crowd that ever got together in Central Kansas" (fig. 111).[128]

The good feelings (and business profits) that came from the 1902 extravaganza were nearly duplicated in 1905 with another heavily promoted gathering. This time the occasion was the annual tournament of the State Firemen's Association. Although the bands were numerous and in good form, and the firemen's races were exciting, something else lifted this day from special to unique for townspeople and the thousand or so outsiders present. Junction City residents had purchased their first automobiles in 1905. As a late addition to the parade, nineteen of the owners (almost all) decided to decorate their already prized Cadillacs, Fords, Glides, Oldsmobiles, Orients, Smiths, and Waynes. Their stately procession up Jefferson Street and down Washington was spoken about for years afterward (fig. 112; compare fig. 11).[129]

The other two community-bonding events were unplanned. Coincidentally, they also took place within the same month in 1903. The first was a visit from President Theodore Roosevelt. Roosevelt did not come specifically to see the town, of course. He was on an extended tour of the West. Having spoken in Saint Louis at the Louisiana Purchase Centennial Exposition, and wanting to visit the Grand Canyon, Yosemite, and other of his favorite places, he was just

110. Ladies' Progressive Reading and Art Club, 1914 (print 2754). This group, like most others of its genre, was primarily a forum for self-education and growth. Its members did not challenge traditional gender roles. African American clubs in Kansas tended to stress art and music, and the Junction City group was no exception, judging from a surviving program. At a meeting hosted by Charity (Mrs. Newton) Aldridge, scripture reading, a vocal solo, and an instrumental solo were interspersed with several committee reports (*Topeka Plaindealer,* July 5, 1912). Members include Mrs. Ira Perkins (left) and Ida Morris (right) in the front row. Valinda White is third from the left in the second row. Ellen Johnson and E. M. McCord stand on the left and right ends, respectively, of the back row.

111. Fourth of July celebration, 1902 (print 855.6). The city's commercial club erected a temporary platform near the intersection of East Seventh Street and Washington for singing and other special events. Onstage is an unknown minstrel group, which was scheduled to perform just before a big finale of fireworks. Pennell was able to take this photograph while standing on his own stairway (compare figs. 11 and 32). The Bartell House is in the background; a Hartford Insurance sign marks the office of Alfred C. Pierce.

112. Leo Loeb's decorated Cadillac, 1905 (print 1563.1). The look on Loeb's face says that all is right with the world. His new automobile, a ten-horsepower model, cost $950, but was beautiful and made him a center of attention. Grace Hubbert sits next to him. Elizabeth Loeb is one of the other passengers. Although the date was a week or so after Labor Day, white obviously was still the proper color (*Junction City Union,* March 10, 1905; Jeffries and Jeffries, *Garden of Eden,* p. 101).

passing through Kansas. Townspeople were nevertheless ecstatic at the prospect, even though the scheduled stop on May 2 was only from 10:50 to 11:05. They built a special speaker's stand near the depot, gave out a thousand flags for schoolchildren to carry, and installed ropes to control the expected crowd. All went as planned. Five thousand people heard a twenty-one-gun salute, listened to a short speech on the righteousness of the recent war in Cuba and the Philippines, and went away feeling invigorated because the most important person in the country had chosen to visit them (fig. 113).[130]

The afterglow from the presidential visit proved to be short-lived. Twenty-seven days after the depot was decked with bunting, its grounds were covered by several feet of water. A five-inch rainstorm on May 28, which fell on ground already saturated by heavy rains the week before, created what a *Union* reporter called "the West's greatest flood." His exaggeration was only slight, for it certainly was the worst in Kansas history up to that time. The Republican River rose first, flooding Grant Avenue by early morning and then washing out the bridge. The Smoky Hill was even more spectacular. It rose five feet in an hour and by noon appeared as "a vast sea" (fig. 114).

The Republican River had flooded its bottomlands north of town fairly regularly over the years, but a big overflow from the Smoky Hill was unexpected. "No one thought of the water rising to [the houses along Price and Monroe Streets], but the flood came up so fast that few were able to get much of their furniture out." Aurora Mills, the Rockwell elevator, and both depots were inundated, and uncounted miles of railroad track and telephone lines were washed away. The Henderson Bridge, south of town, did not survive either. Miraculously, no one drowned in Junction City proper, although seven members of the Daniel Meyers family died in the narrow valley of Clark's Creek. Townspeople were left to their own resources and seemed to draw strength from one another. For nearly two weeks they were cut off from the world. No train could get through from any direction for eleven days, and a month passed before the tracks reopened to the east.[131]

To more fully appreciate the human impact of a flood, or any other event that acts to knit a community together, a series of close-range photographs would be ideal. Pictures of people burying drowned cattle before they could spread disease might lend genuine empathy, for example. So would shots of neighbors who helped one another clean the mud from their homes. This expectation is too much to ask of a studio photographer burdened with bulky equipment, of course. Although we can learn much from Pennell's depictions of houses, fire departments, and clubs, perhaps the closest approach he can offer us to the core of human values is through studies of the key stages in the cycle of life. From the many hundreds of photographs he took of weddings, childhood events, and death, I offer a brief sample (figs. 115–121). They seem a fitting way to close this section. Some of the faces show earnestness, joy, and optimism. Others reveal sadness and even death itself. These qualities are as basic as they come, in Junction City or anywhere else.

113. President Theodore Roosevelt at Junction City, 1903 (print 1164.10). Union Pacific officials were as ecstatic as Junction City residents that the president had chosen to travel this route. They equipped his train with the newest Pullman cars and decorated the engine with bunting, flags, and painted sunflowers. Secretary of War Elihu Root, standing next to Roosevelt, also addressed the crowd. His speech praised Fort Riley and the valor its soldiers had demonstrated in the Spanish-American War (*Junction City Union,* May 8, 1903).

114. The flood of 1903 (print 1028.1). From the distance of the courthouse, the waters look calm. Contemporary newspapers, however, reported that "one by one the buildings commenced floating off" as the flood advanced westward almost to Franklin Street (*Junction City Union,* June 5, 1903). Eighth Street is on the right side of the photograph, Ninth Street in the left center. From left to right along the railroad tracks stand the Union Pacific Depot, the Union Pacific freight house, Aurora Mills, the city power plant, and the Rockwell elevator. This photograph also provides a rare glimpse into the backyards of several houses with their privies, coal sheds, and stables. East Ninth Street contains no commercial development. Its rise as an African American business center was twenty years in the future.

115. The Pauley wedding, 1901 (print 775.6). Birdie May Pauley married Albert W. Buhrer on Thanksgiving Day at the farm home of her parents near Alida, northwest of Junction City. For the event, the family made the house "into a garden with luxuriant evergreen and feathery asparagus" and then served dinner to over 100 guests. The bride's gown is silk, her flowers roses. The groom owned a hardware store in nearby Enterprise, Kansas. Both parents indulged their children. The Pauleys gave a bedroom suite, a set of chairs, a carpet, a rug, and a check for $100. The Buhrers provided a deed for a house, four lots in town, and two carpets (*Junction City Union,* December 6, 1901).

116. Edith Monroe's school group, 1909 (print 2266). Judging from the building walls and windows, this fourth-grade class attended Franklin School at the corner of Third Street and Madison. The percentage of African American children was fairly consistent across all four of the city's elementary schools, a function of that group's dispersed pattern of housing (see map 5). Black stockings and ankle-length black shoes were standard for both girls and boys. Tanned faces suggest that the season was fall.

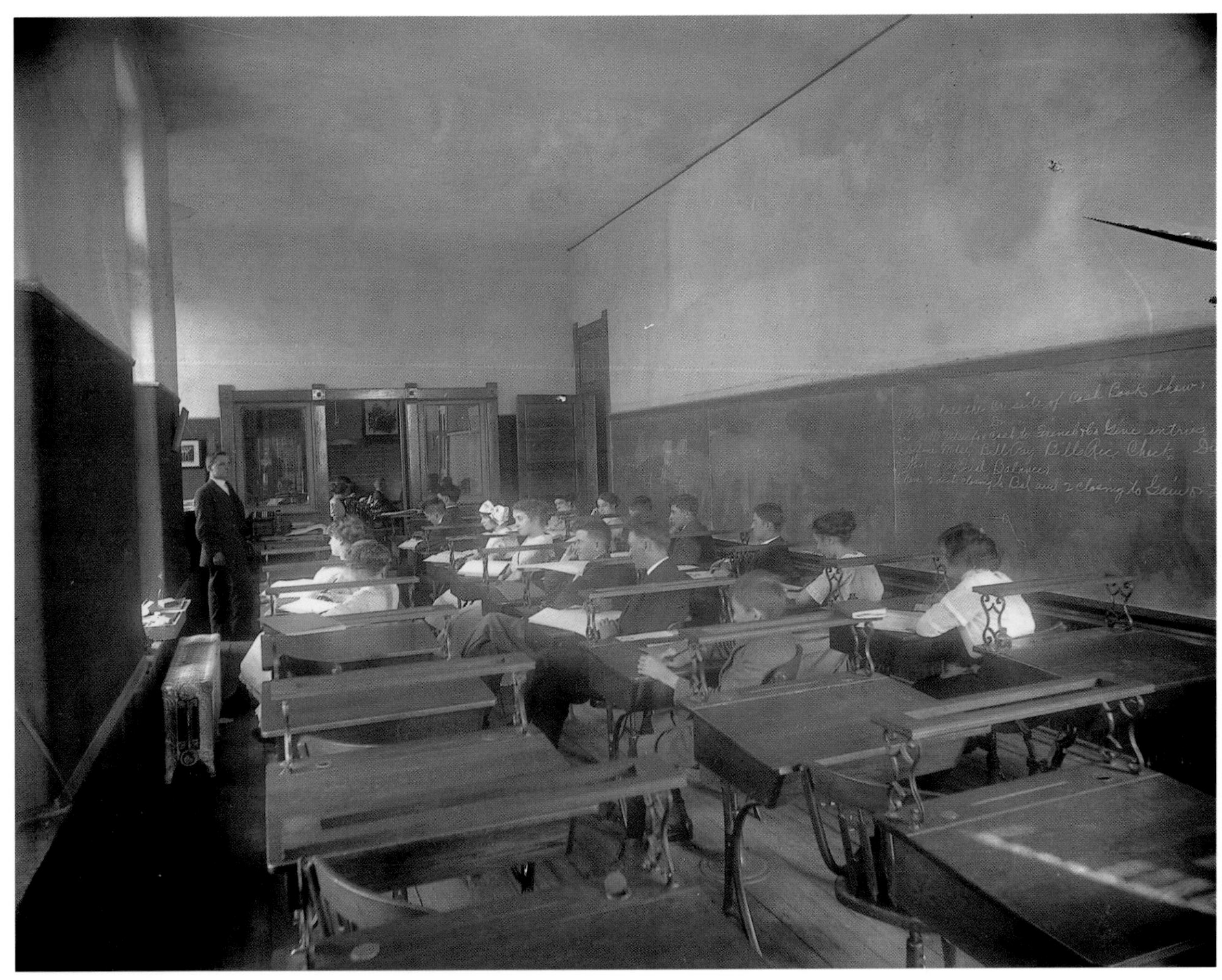

117. Commercial class, 1913 (print 2624). High school was elite education in 1913, a time when only about 10 percent of the American population had earned this diploma. Most schools offered several courses of study, including college preparatory, normal training (i.e., teaching), and commercial. Pennell made a rare trip ten miles west to photograph the commercial classrooms of C. U. Nichols in the basement level of Chapman High School. A serious demeanor is clear from body language and clothing selection. A typewriting classroom is through the far doorway; a calculating machine sits in front. Special slotted boards elevated above the desks are for holding the ledger books used in book-keeping classes (Josselyn, "Survey of Accredited High Schools," p. 209).

118. Football team at Junction City High School, 1901 (print 657). Sports in the school system were just beginning in 1901. As team quarterback Robert J. Ballinger recalled: "We bought our own uniforms, scheduled our own games, solicited money from the businessmen to bring out-of-town teams here and, if we didn't have enough, the coach put up the money, hoping to get it back out of the gate receipts. We knew he didn't, and since he was not paid for coaching, we knew it cost him a good many dollars to keep the team running" (*Junction City Union,* June 24, 1953). In the back row, left to right, are principal T. P. Detamore, Rolla Coryell, Roy Dalton, (?) Walters, and Dr. Fred O'Donnell (the coach). In the middle row are Robert J. Ballinger, Bill Hauserman, Ted Hemenway, Dib Hartshorn, and Blake Ziegler. Seated are Ralph Glick, Herbert Davis, and Bill Campbell.

119. Flanagan's monument, 1898 (print 269.6). After having worked hard to turn a frontier community into a successful city, older Junction City people at the turn of the century expected that their descendants would stay on and enjoy the fruits of their labors. Accordingly, they purchased cemetery lots big enough for a dozen or more burials. Patrick Flanagan's son and granddaughter visited his stone in Saint Mary's Cemetery six years after his death, but neither is now interred beside him. Extended family lots soon disappeared from a mobile America. At Saint Mary's, a different, smaller stone now occupies this spot, and strangers lie next to Flanagan.

120. Augustine baby funeral viewing, 1900 (print 629.1). The death of Orea Augustine three months before her second birthday contributed to a sad set of statistics. Between 15 and 20 percent of the children born in the United States in 1900 died as infants, with another 10 to 15 percent succumbing during childhood. Pennell and other photographers recorded many of these occasions, and they also were called upon for "just-in-case" shots when mothers learned that their children had been exposed to whooping cough, scarlet fever, or another deadly disease. A baby's second summer was the most feared time in the years before refrigeration. This was when he or she likely would be exposed to slightly spoiled food. To counter the problem, many families turned from fresh milk to canned once this product became available (Holt, *Linoleum,* pp. 95–120; Reid, *Hurry Home Wednesday,* pp. 252–58).

121. Dumm's hearse, 1900 (print 638). Partly because death was so common, and partly because dying and funerals regularly took place in homes rather than in specialized facilities, these occasions were accepted more easily in 1900 than now. One of the town's two undertakers, William C. Dumm, could even leave his muddy hearse in the city park without controversy. The black curtains visible were standard for adult funerals; white was substituted for children. Funerals are rich in symbolism. The six urns atop the hearse are traditional icons for wisdom and devotion. The middle casting appears to be an anchor encircled by a crown of laurel leaves. These things symbolize, respectively, the voyage to eternity and eternity itself.

Change

"I was born into a world that ceased to exist almost as soon as I came into it." These words, written by a man who grew up in Michigan during the 1910s, echo true for a generation of Americans. Everybody knows the basic facts that he alludes to: about horses giving way to automobiles, coal-oil lamps to incandescent bulbs, and solitude to ringing telephones. We also know that these technological innovations were accompanied by social change on a major scale, as new ideas circulated at faster and faster speeds. Where we have difficulty, however, is in grasping the process and in envisioning how people of the time understood the events going on about them. "In the first twelve years of my life," the Michigan man continued, "rural America was swept away as completely as though it was a picture on a black board that had been suddenly erased. The technological revolution . . . flooded through the country. It came so suddenly and the changes were so thorough that most people didn't realize that the old way of life had gone."[132] Of all the insights that Joseph Pennell's photographs can reveal, this one of the transition between two worlds is arguably his most significant.

The beginnings of technological change for Junction City occurred in the 1880s with the first telephone service and electrical connections. Cornelius Fogarty added a small generator to his gristmill on the Smoky Hill River, and the Bell telephone monopoly installed a few lines for businesses.[133] For about a decade, however, people regarded these things as no more than expensive novelties. They were not topics of popular discussion, and their usage failed to expand noticeably. Attitudes changed only in the late 1890s, once money began to flow from the expansion of Fort Riley. Then, within a decade, the city went from septic tanks to a municipal sewer system, from individual wells and cisterns to a public waterworks, and from weak kerosene lamps to bright incandescent bulbs and the first of many new electrical appliances.

The movement seems to have started in 1896, when John K. Wright and Augustus Bartell decided that their Bartell House hotel needed a sewer. In exchange for an offer to turn their tiling over to the city at cost whenever a larger system might be established, officials let the men dig some 3,250 feet down Washington Street to Second and then east into the Smoky Hill River. By 1899, a group of home owners had constructed an extension up the alley between Third and Fourth Streets to serve that residential area. Similar initiatives followed, and in 1906, the council decided that the time had come for a comprehensive municipal system. All was complete the following summer: thirteen miles of pipe at a cost of $80,000. Sewers do not make good photographic subjects, but in conjunction with a new municipal water system that had been installed a few years earlier, they soon rendered privies a rare sight.[134]

More photogenic than sewers, and seen by the newspapers of the time as a far greater accomplishment, were advances in the generation of electricity. This product, the editors argued, should now be seen as a tool that could affect business in a positive way. The new attitude seems to have been initiated by Cornelius Fogarty, who realized that his dam on the Smoky Hill could produce electricity as well as flour. When the city accepted his offer to install streetlights in the downtown area in 1897, merchants found that shoppers stayed later and purchased more goods. The owners responded by adding lights to their show windows and more for their interiors—so many, in fact, that Fogarty had to buy new generating equipment the next year.[135]

Fogarty died before he could reap the financial rewards of his investment, and city officials decided that they should take charge of their own electrical future. A new and much bigger plant was needed, they reasoned, one closer to the city and adjacent to the railroad so as to obtain coal to run modern dynamos. They selected a site on East Eighth Street next to Aurora Mills, drew up a set of ambitious plans, and, without hesitation, issued bonds for an unprecedented cost of $114,300. When the new powerhouse was completed in August 1901, they called it "the greatest and most important enterprise which has been undertaken in this community" (figs. 122 and 123).[136]

With the opening of the plant came another, much larger increase in electrical usage. It happened so fast that a reporter from the *Union* was almost flabbergasted:

> Nearly or quite all of the business portion of the city doubled the number of incandescent lights in use . . . and a score of the smaller establishments, where few or no lights had been used, at once made application for suitable lighting. The Daily Union office may almost be taken as an example, showing the growth of the business. This office jumped from two to ten, and now is at a loss to know how a fewer number could possibly meet the requirements. The demand for lights in the various residence portions of the city [which had no service before] has been equal to that coming from the business houses. Thus far a dozen or more of the best homes of the city have been lighted. This feature of the business is growing as rapidly as the company has been able to care for it. In two years it is probable that three-fourths of the better homes of the city will be using electric lights.[137]

With all the enthusiasm, no one seemed to notice or mind that Washington Street had become a jungle of stark wooden poles and dangling wires (see figs. 11, 16, and 17).

Accompanying the obsession with electric lights were the related miracles of an electrically powered system of streetcars and telephones. The trolley installation was part of the same grand plan that produced the powerhouse. In fact, the official name of the plant was the Junction City Electric Railway, Light and Ice Company. Newspaper reporters failed to give the new transportation service quite the coverage they did lighting, possibly because the idea of building such a line had been discussed since 1886. It was highly successful, however, a pure business venture to encourage soldiers to bring their money to town more frequently. Charging ten cents for the four-mile trip from downtown (the car barn was on Washington Street across from the park) to Waters Hall on the post, the line averaged 500 passengers a day. Its cars ran every half hour from five in the morning until eleven at night (fig. 124). The fact that such traffic meant a substantial reduction in the manure droppings along city streets, along with increases in merchant revenue, was never commented on publicly.[138]

A surge in telephone adoption paralleled that of electric lights. A reporter in 1897 noted that linemen "have been and are busy" with installations in the courthouse, several businesses, and a few residences. By 1899, the subscriber list had grown to 110, and the Bell company had installed three special lines for long-distance calls. Telephones moved perceptually from a

122. Power plant building, 1901 (print 807.11). Described as "one of the largest and best equipped" facilities in the state, this T-shaped building had three main divisions. The seventy-five-foot smokestack marks the boiler room and storage area for coal, which was served by a spur from the MKT Railroad. A big generator room is nearest the camera, and the wing on the right housed ice-making equipment, a related enterprise of the company. H. H. Ziegler designed the layout. Pennell's view is to the southwest, with the Rockwell elevator visible near the chimney (*Junction City Union,* August 16, 1901).

123. Generator room in the power plant, 1901 (print 807.9). Local people had never seen machinery on the scale of the three huge engines and four dynamos housed in their new powerhouse. They came often to visit. Each engine produced 250 horsepower, and the dynamos had the capacity for 3,000 incandescent bulbs and 140 arc lights (*Junction City Union,* August 16, 1901).

124. Streetcar, 1901 (print 701). Strictly speaking, a trolley is a linear device that collects current from an overhead wire and transmits it to the motor of an electric vehicle. The name soon was applied to the vehicles themselves. The Junction City line began business with two identical cars plus a pair of trailers to handle especially busy periods. These cars are stubby compared with later models (see fig. 12), and could carry only twelve passengers apiece. A motorman maneuvered the control handle from the front platform (the right end in the photograph). The system of cars and tracks cost $51,500 plus another $5,300 for a bridge over the Republican River (see maps 2 and 4). Service ended in February 1934 in favor of buses (Chandler, *Trolley through the Countryside,* pp. 102–28).

luxury item to a necessity the next year, when the city awarded a competing franchise to an independent company led by H. P. Wareham of Manhattan. Wareham promised to drop business rates from $36 a year to $24, and residential rates from $30 to $15. Immediately, everybody wanted an installation.[139]

Pragmatic Junction City residents initially rationalized their purchases carefully. "A telephone in the house often saves lives and property," one man wrote. With a telephone, "you can call the physician, you can call the fire department, . . . you can be in immediate touch with the entire community." Less than a year later, the transition was complete: "With the city full of phones, and most residents connected, people will wonder how they have been living without one." Old oak switchboards had to be replaced with bigger models on a yearly basis, and by 1906, even most farmers were connected on party lines (fig. 125). Joseph Thoes, in Wingfield Township, was fined $25 that year for using profane language on the phone. His case was an easy decision, since "authorities had the names of four women who had the receivers down and who were listening."[140]

Sewers, electric lights, and telephones were all in place in Junction City before technology began to affect transportation in a fundamental way. Collectively, these earlier advances of the late 1890s had made life easier for the people who could afford them, but they had not changed the fundamental pace and essential geography of everyday existence. A thousand things, including the spacing of schools and churches, the viability of hamlets, and the number of rural patients a doctor could visit in a day, were determined by the speed of horse-drawn transportation. So were the sizes of farms, the crowds a local merchant might hope to attract for a sale, and a host of more personal matters such as the range of contacts a man might encounter in a day or a lifetime. When writers describe the nineteenth century with the epigram "the horse is king," they mean far more than an affection for a particular animal.

The transportation revolution in Junction City and elsewhere occurred in stages. The 1890s, as Pennell's record makes clear, was the last decade to be dominated by the horse. A transition took place over the next fifteen years, with automobiles present for most of the time but not yet widely available or reliable. Bicycles actually were the primary topic of discussion during the early years of this period. Gradually, road conditions, rather than mechanical problems, became the factor limiting wider use of the vehicles that people now sometimes called cars. It was not until 1920 or so that all the elements were in place for independent long-distance travel.

Horse-drawn transportation, as one might expect from a system that had been evolving for centuries, was quite sophisticated by 1900. Carriages—that is, vehicles designed for transporting people—came in many styles. Light, one-horse models ranged from two-wheeled runabouts or gigs to standard four-wheeled buggies (see fig. 74) to elegant enclosed broughams with separate drivers' seats. Of the two-horse carriages, phaetons were the models of choice, especially those with folding tops (fig. 126), but the possibilities were many. Young ladies could tell much about the financial status and degree of ardor of their gentlemen callers by the type of rigs they rented from the local livery stable.

125. Miss Crook (left) and Miss Mickey at the Wareham-Dewey switchboard, 1905 (print 1518B). Operating from a room above Shaw's general mercantile store at 119 West Seventh Street, these young women mechanically connected Junction City residents with one another and the world. When a person initiating a call picked up his or her phone, one of the disks on the switchboard would drop down (they are called "drops"). The operator then would plug in one end of a drop cord, flip a switch, and ask the caller what number was wanted. Next, she would take the other end of her cord and plug it into the number requested. Finally, she would ring the person on that line with a ring switch (the knobs closest to the operators). A typical farm telephone number, 12-F-21, meant a combination of two long rings and one short one on farm line twelve.

126. Erica Dahlstrom and Margaret Gordon on West Seventh Street, 1901 (print 789). The Dahlstroms were a Milford family, which meant that Erica had at least an hour's drive into Junction City. Her team, a nicely matched pair, are wearing blinders to keep city distractions to a minimum. Note the hitching post at the curb and the sign for Garland stoves beside the door of Muenzenmayer's Hardware. The Muenzenmayers stocked a different brand from their rival John Davidson (see fig. 24).

Carriages were a graceful, light, and relatively fast means of transportation. Narrow, large-diameter wheels helped provide these qualities, but such wheels also cut deep ruts into the dirt roads whenever it rained. Shoppers and visitors alike were keenly aware of this problem, and since dirt roads were nearly universal, they always kept an eye on the sky while going about any activity away from home. Muddy roads easily could slow the pace of travel from fifteen miles per hour to three or four and often meant no travel at all. People who needed to transport heavy loads would likely wait for dry conditions, but they also made sure they had wide wheels on their wagons (fig. 127).

Carriages and wagons did not have the roads to themselves in 1900. Leaning against the Muenzenmayer building in figure 126 are a pair of bicycles. Careful inspection also reveals such vehicles in many other Pennell photographs (see figs. 17, 18, 23, 31, 34, 54, 83, and 90). These machines first came into Junction City shortly after 1889 as part of a national enthusiasm for a new design called a "safety" bicycle. It featured two equal-sized wheels and pneumatic tires, which made riding much easier than on the earlier high-wheeled models. People loved bicycles for the sense of freedom they provided and did not seem to be inhibited at all by the absence of a braking system. Enough local owners existed by 1893 to organize the Junction City Cycling Club, and three years later, hardware stores began to feature them in their advertisements. That same year, Ernest Wetzig opened a shop completely devoted to bicycle sales and repairs.[141]

Bicycles are credited with revolutionizing women's attitudes toward exercise and helping to bring an end to the age of tight corsetting (fig. 128). They made bloomers and shorter skirts credible options for attire, provided a means for young people to escape the eyes of their elders, and served as regular transportation for many workers (fig. 129).[142] Single women especially valued the independence a bicycle afforded them, since the males in the family tended to control the horse and carriage.

Bicycles also set the stage in many ways for the successful development of the automobile. On the technical side, bicycle manufacturers were the first to create pneumatic tires, wire wheels, ball and roller bearings, the differential axle, variable-speed transmissions, and steel tube frames. Riders, as they began to race and tour on their new machines, printed the first widely distributed road maps and initiated efforts to mark routes between towns and to improve overall road conditions. Abilene wheelmen were part of this latter effort as early as 1899, as they planned a group excursion to Junction City. Most important of all, perhaps, bicycles planted the seed of desire in people for independent long-distance travel. Trains, wonders that they were, began to be seen as restrictive. The stage was set for an engine-powered vehicle of some sort that could extend the range of a bicycle.[143]

Junction City's first automobile arrived in early March 1905. It was a Cadillac, purchased on speculation by the Muenzenmayer Hardware Company. This choice was based on the model's popularity in Kansas City (where Cadillac outsold other brands twenty to one) and a demonstration "that all kinds of grades look alike to a Cadillac." The price of $950 was steep,

127. Dumm's load of furniture, 1903 (print 1108). East Eighth Street was a busy thoroughfare. In addition to the trolley cars that ran every half hour, it was the route merchants and draymen took to pick up merchandise from the freight house of the Union Pacific Railroad. The street was one of the first in town to be macadamized because of this traffic. According to the sign on the smaller wagon, Dumm's furniture store had a telephone by 1903. The courthouse is on the left.

128. Jim Miller's house, 1899 (print 468.9). Miller (a brakeman on the railroad) and his family provide a classic display of the transportation of their time. Their main vehicle is a surrey, distinctive with its flat bottom and rigid roof (fringed, in this case, just as in the song). Both young women have "wheels," machines of personal freedom that were adopted by females nearly as fast as by males, or perhaps even faster.

129. Bush on bicycle, 1902 (print 913.1). Colby Bush used a bicycle as an integral part of the messenger and dray business he operated out of his home at 432 West Sixth Street. Like other models of the time, his vehicle lacked both brakes and fenders. The photograph looks west down Seventh Street from Washington. The First National Bank is on the right, the clock tower of the opera house in the background. On the left is a watering wagon, which was employed to control dust on city streets.

but Muenzenmayer said that he hoped to sell five or six of them during the year. The Muenzenmayer venture was imitated three weeks later by Fundis and Good, a rival hardware dealer, which purchased a $1,125 "Glide machine" from the manufacturer in Peoria, Illinois.[144]

The two display models generated intense discussion on Washington Street and a strong desire for ownership. After only a few weeks, and almost en masse, a large group of leading businessmen each decided to purchase a machine. They studied the advertising literature that suddenly had appeared everywhere, and they selected a wide assortment of makers. Lumberman George Moses opted for a Cadillac, Dr. William S. Yates for an Oldsmobile, Waldo Tyler of Aurora Mills a Wayne, and MKT agent Charles H. Bumstead a Ford (fig. 130). Altogether, twenty-three vehicles had been sold by the end of July. Besides styling, the biggest issue was whether to go for a lighter (and cheaper) model or a heavier one that might hold up better on winter roads when ruts were frozen in place.[145]

At first, people treated their new automobiles almost as if they were horses. In July 1905, for example, when the Reust brothers opened the first local garage for the machines, the basic idea was to keep everybody's vehicles at that location. "They will deliver the cars at residences and will call for them when the owners so desire," said a reporter. "A man will be kept at the garage day and night. Doctors' automobiles will be delivered or called for any time." At least three of the owners failed to take advantage of this service, because their vehicles were damaged badly in late November when water froze in their radiators.[146]

Newspapers stopped recording each new purchase after the first season of activity. Instead, reports covered the establishment of new agencies for the sale of cars by specific makers (fig. 131) and the overland trips that small caravans of the new vehicles had begun to attempt. The first long trek, apparently, was a two-week, 500-mile adventure to southeastern Kansas undertaken by the families of William C. Dumm and Bert Tyler.

Owners loved to test the speed and agility of their machines and often tore along roads with abandon. This activity was tolerated by most wives but feared by people who drove horses. When Jacob Meyer's team was frightened by an unknown car northeast of town and he was thrown from his wagon and run over by a wheel, the neighbors were outraged. Mrs. John Cameron wrote a fiery letter to the *Union* about "the automobile juggernauts." These people have made nine-tenths of the farm women too afraid to venture onto the roads, she argued. "Can the business men of Junction City afford to allow twenty-five residents of their city drive the farmers with their products and trade to the small towns and the mail-order houses of large cities, which it surely will if there is not some provision made for their safety."[147] Mrs. Cameron hit the automobile owners where it hurt. To her proposal that cars be banned for two days each week, they responded with a carefully worded apology. Courtesy should prevail, they agreed, and they promised that whenever a person would raise a hand as a signal for "a scary horse," the auto driver would stop until the horse had passed safely.[148]

The Meyer incident contributed to a different and more channeled approach to testing automobile skills—endurance runs. When two men passed through town in August 1907 while attempting to break the speed record between Kansas City and Denver, the excitement was

130. Charles Bumstead's Ford, 1906 (print 1701). Bumstead was the local agent for the Missouri, Kansas and Texas Railway and chose to be photographed on the platform of his depot (the rival Union Pacific station is in the background). His car is a Model C. This was a modification of Henry Ford's original design, the Model A, and sold for $850 when it was first put on the market in September 1904. The Model C featured pneumatic tires, a squeeze-bulb horn, and kerosene lamps. The fuel tank is under the hood. Note also that the steering wheel is on the right, the standard position until Ford moved it in 1908 for his first Model T. The sight of a woman at the wheel was most unusual in 1906. The explanation here might be courtship. Bumstead married Lucy Marrs in 1909 (*Junction City Union,* November 5, 1909).

131. Wetzig auto shop, 1908 (print 2036). Ernest and Herman Wetzig came to Junction City from Winkler, Kansas, and opened a bicycle shop in 1896. In 1905 they acquired the rights to sell Reo automobiles in a five-county area. From their building at 912 North Washington they sold twenty of the new machines in 1907. In 1909 they set a franchise record with thirty-five sales from January through May (*Junction City Union,* September 15, 1905; April 10, 1908; June 4, 1909). Reos were quality automobiles manufactured by Ransom Olds beginning in 1904. A small runabout sits on the left; the others are touring cars.

palpable. A month later, the Kansas City Automobile Club provided a similar but more realistic model for adventure when it put Junction City on its route for a three-day endurance tour of northeastern Kansas. Within days, local people agreed that they should stage an event of their own. It became known as the Lyric Cup Run when Ira Bermant, owner of the Lyric Theater, donated a trophy for the winner (fig. 132).[149]

Automobile enthusiasm started fast in Junction City and never slowed. Men all seemed entranced by the smell of oil and the talk of horsepower. Women supported the adventure as well, even though they were largely excluded from the garage, but their reasons were not entirely altruistic. With the men giddy over the machines, women often had the family horse and carriage at their complete disposal for the first time.[150] By 1910, poor road conditions were seen as the main limitation to continued expansion. Roads could be improved, of course, but marshaling the effort and money to do so would require a united front throughout the county. Farmers, who were still largely without automobiles in 1910, had to be convinced that good roads were not something that would benefit only their city cousins.

The road problems in Geary County were repeated across the nation. They were addressed beginning about 1900 by a cooperative effort known as the good-roads movement. As part of this, Colonel W. H. Moore toured the state in January 1905. At Junction City and elsewhere, he argued that good roads benefited everybody and urged legislation at the state level for funds. As time passed and nothing immediate came of the colonel's exhortation, people began to focus their efforts locally. Editors enthusiastically reported the rise in automobile ownership among farmers, city officials constructed "drags" to smooth the main entry roads six miles out into the county, and the commercial club raised money to reward road overseers who could show especially good results. The dragging of principal rural roads became a Kansas law in 1909, with townships required to pay up to $5 per mile annually for this work. To ensure that this edict was seen in positive terms, the Junction City merchants sponsored Good Roads Days in both 1911 and 1912. They financed a banquet for all workers, awarded numerous prizes, and hired Pennell to record the events (figs. 133 and 134).[151]

Within the city, council members experimented with several different street surfaces in the decade from 1910 to 1919: oil, macadam bounded by concrete gutters and curbs, and brick. The first concrete pavement came in December 1914, when officials took bids for a narrow center slab flanked by macadam on South Washington. The leap to full concrete construction occurred in 1917. Extremely heavy traffic at Fort Riley during World War I prompted federal officials to authorize eighteen miles of new pavement in and around the post. With this came contractors with specialized equipment who soon applied their skills to West Eighth, Washington, and then other city streets (fig. 135).[152]

As automobiles, telephones, and other technological marvels worked their way into the fabric of American society in the 1910s, the pace of change increased everywhere in the country. Junction City, however, received an extra jolt of economic adrenalin in 1917 when the United States entered World War I and officials named Fort Riley as a major center for mobilization. Virtually overnight came the announcement that up to 70,000 recruits would be sent to Kansas and that a whole new encampment would have to be built. A contract awarded in May to the Fuller Construction Company of New York called for 123 new barracks, 96

132. Samuel Ziegler's E.M.F. Studebaker at the Lyric Cup run, 1909 (print 2240). The second Lyric Cup contest, on October 25–26, attracted eighteen entries for a 250-mile trip that included lunch the first day at Lindsborg, an overnight stay at Hutchinson, and lunch the second day at Marion. Entrants departed at fifteen-minute intervals and were to average fifteen miles per hour. Charles C. Shoffner's Cadillac and George H. Flower's Overland were declared co-winners because they reported the fewest mechanical breakdowns. Ziegler and his brother owned the local Studebaker agency. "E.M.F. 30" on the running board refers to the Everitt-Metzger-Flanders Company of Detroit, which had a brief joint venture with Studebaker before being absorbed in 1908. The "30" is the horsepower of this model, which sold for $1,250. Competitors insisted that E.M.F. referred to either "Every Mechanical Fault" or "Every Morning Fix" (*Junction City Union,* October 15, 1909; October 22, 1909; October 29, 1909; Corle, *John Studebaker,* pp. 240–43).

133. Good Roads Day, 1912 (print 2584.9). For a special day of work and celebration on May 14, leaders from Junction City's commercial club selected captains to oversee dragging and repair activities on eleven routes. They also invited the several hundred workers to a banquet afterward. Canyon Road, a main route across Fort Riley, had the biggest turnout, with forty-one men and twenty-seven teams. The drags used were based on a design by local farmer Peter Gfeller (*Junction City Union,* July 3, 1908; April 25, 1912; May 16, 1912).

134. Good Roads Day, 1911 (print 2464.7). According to W. S. Gearhart, the state highway engineer, roads should be dragged slowly, with one's team at a walk. The process should be repeated after every rain and in all seasons and, ideally, should create a twelve-inch crown at the center for drainage (*Junction City Union,* April 18, 1912). A newly dragged road could be a thing of beauty and might even attract some well-dressed city folk for an inspection. Osage orange trees line this road, an effective fence when kept pruned back (as these are) to encourage side branching.

135. Paving mixer, 1919 (print 3111). When the Junction City firm of Ziegler and Dalton landed a highway contract from the state for $220,520, it purchased the biggest and latest equipment available (*Junction City Union,* June 26, 1919). Their self-propelled paving mixer, manufactured by the Koehring Machine Company of Milwaukee, is fairly simple in design. Cement is loaded into a hopper, which is then raised to dump the material into a central drum-shaped mixer (the photograph shows the hopper in the raised position on the left side of the machine). After water is added through the hose visible in the foreground and the mixing is completed, the concrete slush is poured into a bucket (next to the man in dark overalls). The bucket, in turn, slides along a boom to wherever the mixture is required. The work site is the 900-block of North Washington.

bathhouses, 69 mess halls, and much more. Everything was to be wood frame in the interest of time, the site was to be Ogden Flats (about three miles northeast of the main post), and all was to be completed by the end of summer. By June, the estimate for the number of new buildings needed was up to 3,000, the contract had been rewritten, and 10,000 laborers were on the job. When the first recruits arrived in September, they found stark but functional quarters bearing the name of Camp Funston (figs. 136 and 137).[153]

Junction City people quickly found themselves unbelievably busy. First construction workers and then soldiers and soldiers' families came to town. Plans for a community building were among the earliest to materialize, a large structure across from the park on Sixth Street. This would supplement the services available at the Salvation Army's new center and demonstrate appreciation for the young men's sacrifices (fig. 138). This altruistic gesture was soon followed by a series of pragmatic business ventures: a new hotel on East Seventh Street, a military shop by Woolf Brothers, theaters, and a wholesale grocery house by the S. E. Lux Mercantile Company. Rents skyrocketed. Small storefronts that used to bring $40 dollars a week now went for $150, and someone offered to buy out a lease for $3,000 cash. A decent house rented for $100 a month, and one reporter even claimed that "the 'bon ton' of Junction will live under the young elms at the country club east of town this summer, while their homes in town are bringing in gold dollars."[154]

The war ended almost as suddenly as it began. Rents soon came back to normal, and some of the new businesses closed, but the town would never be the same. Its citizens had sampled a bigger world than they had known before. The city was larger as well, and its infrastructure more complete. Anna Murray's parents, for example, had constructed a new bakery that more than doubled their capacity, so they embarked on a wholesale business that made efficient use of this size (see fig. 107). George and Walter Rockwell, among others, had invested in the new, large-capacity motor trucks that had been developed as part of the war effort (fig. 139). These not only altered the appearance of the local streetscape but, by eroding the railroads' monopoly on the transportation of heavy goods, also began to modify the whole locational geography of business and industry.[155]

If the same person who had taken the hypothetical walk along Washington Street with Pennell in 1905 were to return just after the war, he or she would sense definite change (fig. 140). Although many of the stores had the same ownership, the noise level had increased dramatically. Paving, which brought with it a much appreciated improvement in sanitation, also intensified rather than absorbed the sounds of hoofs and heels. Automobiles were everywhere, their inadequate mufflers a major contributor to the din, and their numbers and speed enough to discourage playful groups of donkeys and children (see fig. 14).

A closer look at the built landscape would reveal hints of a new aesthetic. The owners of the Bartell House added not only an entire third story on its south side, but also a pair of oriels (compare figs. 12 and 141). Larger lettering ("Flower's Confectionery") and projecting signs ("Bartell House") are sure indicators that people were now passing by at much faster speeds in their increasingly sophisticated motorcars. When the directors of the First National Bank decided to erect a new building on the old site in 1913, they not only expanded one lot to the north but also employed stylish new materials and designs (compare figs. 15 and 142). A

136. Barracks at Camp Funston, 1917 (print 2959.10). This was one of 123 identical buildings constructed rapidly in the summer of 1917. All were set on concrete posts, and none included shower or eating facilities. Separate units were maintained for black and white recruits. After the war, this and 800 other buildings were sold at public auction. Barracks brought between $151 and $325 apiece (*Junction City Union,* May 24, 1917; July 5, 1917; August 18, 1921).

137. Medical Officers' Training Camp, 1917 (print 2959.23). In addition to preparing recruits for the regular army at Camp Funston, Fort Riley also hosted the nation's largest training program for doctors. Each group stayed for three months at a site just east and southeast of the post hospital (the present-day post headquarters). Thirteen hundred volunteers were here in September 1917 (Pride, *History of Fort Riley,* p. 278; *Junction City Union,* September 27, 1917; Eliot, "Making Medical Officers").

138. Salvation Army Service Club, 1919 (print 3112/3113). The Salvation Army established a major presence in Junction City in 1909 when it constructed a stone "citadel" at 117 East Seventh Street. This was a large building with a fifteen-foot ceiling and a seating capacity of 300. When the war came, it was a simple matter to create a special section for the soldiers (*Junction City Union,* April 23, 1909).

139. Rockwell's truck, 1919 (print 3048). In 1917, the B. Rockwell Merchandise and Grain Company purchased four "six hundred capacity" vehicles from the Republic Motor Truck Company, primarily to haul supplies to Fort Riley. Republics were manufactured in Alma, Michigan, from 1913 through 1929, and these four were reported to "get over the ground, give no trouble, and have the carrying capacity" (*Junction City Union,* July 5, 1917). The truck sits here on East Eighth Street, beside the Rockwell store. The big barrel contains oysters.

140. Washington Street, 1920–1921 (print 3299). The anchor buildings at the corner of Seventh Street did not change in the first two decades of the twentieth century: the First National Bank on the left, and Miller Drugs on the right. At least one bicyclist also remains as a reminder of the past (the blur in front of the drugstore), as does the trolley line. This landscape is now clearly dominated by automobiles, however, with big signs to catch the motorist's eye. The car in the right foreground, a 1918 Dodge, is easily identifiable by its six-panel rear window. General John Pershing used a similar 1916 model in his campaign against Pancho Villa.

141. Bartell House, 1920–1921 (print 3319). Besides paving, perhaps the biggest changes made to Washington Street between 1905 and 1920 involved lighting and utility poles. The ponderous cedar posts obvious in figs. 9–17 are gone, and the telephone and electrical wires they carried were either buried or moved to adjacent alleys. In 1917 city officials installed more graceful "Bates expanded steel truss" standards to carry street signs and 200-watt nitrogen lights. The poles also extend higher to serve as supports for trolley wiring (*Junction City Union,* August 30, 1917).

142. First National Bank, 1913 (print 2684). Conservative neoclassical styling, most obvious here in eight Corinthian pilasters, was the most common choice for banks constructed in the 1910s and 1920s. With $200,000 in capital, First National president Thomas B. Kennedy had a right to feel proud. His taste for cool elegance continued into the interior. According to one report, "the walls, pilasters, and ceiling beams are finished in old ivory, the counters are built of mahogany and English-vein Italian marble, while the wainscoting is of Colorado Yale marble" (*Junction City Republic,* special industrial issue, July 1915).

143. Standard Oil station, 1918 (print 2967). Standard Oil completely dominated its competition early in the twentieth century, controlling 85 percent of the petroleum market in the United States in 1911. It also opened the country's first filling station (1907) and was the first to use uniform designs and color schemes to promote customer identification and loyalty. This is one of the company's "house with canopy" models, designed for placement in residential areas. Parked at the station is a gasoline delivery truck. It was one of several hundred "Patriot" vehicles purchased by Standard from the Hebb Motor Company of Havelock, Nebraska. Hebb built truck bodies and installed them on Ford Model T chassis. Hebb's success led Ford to enter the truck business himself in 1917 (Jakle and Sculle, *Gas Station,* pp. 131–41; McConnell, *Great Cars,* pp. 89–120).

structural steel frame instead of the traditional Fort Riley limestone allowed much of the frontage to be plate glass. They also made extensive use of terra-cotta, a glazed clayware that had just become fashionable, especially for the building's grand cap above the entablature, some fifty feet in the air.[156]

Besides seeing examples of structural steel, terra-cotta, and (slightly later) aluminum and glass block used in the construction of buildings, a visitor to Junction City in 1920 would find several totally new categories of business and radically new designs for others. Most evident, perhaps, if only for their number, were service stations and garages (fig. 143). Although gasoline obviously had been sold locally since the first cars arrived in 1905, the earliest enterprise to specialize in this product and to use the filling-station label appeared in 1914 at the corner of Seventh and Jefferson. Josiah C. Rodgers sold gasoline there for the Cudahy Refining Company at 10.8 cents per gallon. Standard Oil installed a station shortly thereafter at Fifth and Washington and added a second in 1917 at Thirteenth and Washington.[157]

New ideas percolated into town about housing and entertainment as well. Ornate, formal homes with their parlors and pump organs were challenged by sprawling, deliberately informal bungalows. These innovative designs, which had their inspiration in India, Japan, and California, hugged the earth. The ends of their rafters were exposed as a sign of functionalism, their interiors were open and light, and their front doors led directly into living areas, not hallways. Salesman Frank Smith built the first such house in Junction City on South Madison Street in 1909, doing the design work himself. A *Union* reporter admired its daring "block and peg effect." More significant, his words urging an inspection trip "to those who have often wished for a little bungalow and who have never been able to get a good idea of what a real one is like" summarized a more general attitude about many things on the cusp of change.[158]

Movie theaters arrived in town with great anticipation, especially a grandiose one called the Columbia in 1917 (fig. 144). Motion pictures were not brand new, for they had been shown for several years at the opera house and elsewhere as part of an entertainment mix. This art form was just about to come into its own in 1917, however, and having tens of thousands of soldiers nearby made Junction City an ideal spot for a new theater designed with film specifically in mind. The location of the Columbia was much discussed as well, because its site at the southeastern corner of Tenth and Washington represented an abrupt extension of the business district.

The Tenth Street location of the Columbia was determined almost completely by the presence of the Union Pacific depot on that street. Once railroad officials announced a fare of only fifteen cents for the trip from post to town (versus twenty-five cents from post to Manhattan) and businessmen observed soldiers by the hundreds walking between the station and downtown, the geographic principle of intervening opportunity was obvious. The Columbia's owners attached a confectionery store and a barbershop to their building to intercept some of this lucrative trade. Other investors erected a fifty-room frame building they called the Rush Hotel on Tenth near Monroe, and city officials decided to place a second community building there as well, at the corner of Franklin.[159]

144. Columbia Theatre, 1920 (print 3210). H. B. Shanberg, an entrepreneur from Kansas City, had built several other theaters before the Columbia and thought on a large and futuristic scale. His auditorium sat 2,200 people (second only to the Forum in Wichita when the Columbia opened in September 1917), and he utilized fashionable mission styling with gray stucco walls and a red tile roof. Numerous floodlights and large signage, including huge letters suspended above Washington Street, show that he understood the automobile age as well (*Junction City Union,* July 19, 1917; September 27, 1917). The feature movie in early June 1920, when Pennell came by, was a $500,000 production called *The Virgin of Stamboul.* It was advertised as follows: "Thundering across the desert on a stallion shod with fire, the virgin rode at the head of the wild Black Horse Troop to the rescue of her American soldier lover. A mighty photodrama as human as the call of the virgin's heart—as rich with romance and mystery as a shuttered harem" (*Junction City Union,* June 3, 1920).

Many books have been written about the impact of automobiles and other technological innovations on the American landscape and psyche. Among these agents of change, the new motion pictures that flickered before people's eyes in the Columbia and its downtown companion theater, the Cozy, are the most underappreciated. Whether Priscilla Dean as "The Virgin of Stamboul," Mary Pickford, or Lionel Barrymore, these actors offered exciting new possibilities for behavior and dress to every child or adult with an admission fee of eleven or twenty-two cents, respectively. We can see some of the results in Pennell's later photographs of buildings and landscapes, but they come through most clearly and personally in his portraits of individuals.

An appropriate way to close this discussion of life in Junction City between 1895 and 1920 is a comparison of two women, one dressed in a manner typical of the years prior to about 1914, and the other representative of the style that had become dominant by 1920 (figs. 145 and 146). Formality and restraint are perhaps the best descriptors for the earlier portrait. The strength of these two forces was demonstrated nicely in the 1890s, when a few young women in town began to challenge them by wearing bloomers for their bicycle rides. Helen Hemenway, writing in a special issue of the *Republic,* summed up the position of the establishment as follows:

> Men need not be alarmed at the prospect of this fashion becoming the established thing. . . . There are thousands of women who will never adopt the . . . garment because of the discomfort of the sharp criticism made upon their appearance. . . . The average woman would rather look well than feel comfortable at any time.[160]

A transition away from a studied matronly model to a new ideal of looser and more relaxed clothes had begun to occur in larger cities by about 1908, but not in Junction City and other smaller towns. Again, this fact was aptly illustrated by a particular incident—"the flurry" created by a visitor to the Bartell House that year:

> Wearing a gown that staggered the modest—one of those famous sheaths with a princess effect—there she was. As she stood at the counter using the phone, it gave local reporters with the rest of the inquisitive ones, a chance to take a look all around. Of course, a reporter is a sort of privileged character around town, and if he did linger a little longer than others, looking at the effect on the left side, nothing would be said. There it was, the famous slit, and it wasn't buttoned either.[161]

Thinner figures who wore brassieres rather than corsets began to appear in the advertisements of local newspapers in 1911; they became the dominant models by 1914. Then, after an article announced that "skirts will clear the ground from six to twelve inches" for the 1916 season, the changeover came rapidly. Open necks replaced high collars even for middle-age women, and elaborate hats perched atop mounds of long hair yielded to simple bands that accentuated tresses that had been bobbed and curled. Youth was now the idealization, not matronly decorum. With it all came increased freedom of movement and, perhaps, of thought as well.

145. Mrs. Harry Montgomery and son, 1908 (print 2021). Fannie Fern Sheffer married Harry E. Montgomery on September 10, 1902, in Neosho, Missouri. She moved to Junction City immediately thereafter, where her husband coedited the *Union* with his father, John. Harry and Fern's son, John D., would later continue this editorship.

146. Alma Sanders, 1922 (print 3386). Alma, the older daughter of Fred and Clara Sanders, was twenty years old at the time of her photograph. The family lived at 821 West Eleventh Street, and her father worked as a cement contractor.

Pennell, like Moses, was allowed a glimpse into the promised land of sheath dresses and reliable automobiles. He could see that fashions in 1922 were less restrictive than before, but exactly how the bombardment of other new ideas from the outside world would affect the people of Junction City was still uncertain. Would local merchants still be able to compete successfully once people were able to drive into Topeka easily? How would the citizenry accept the army's decision that year to reorganize the famous Ninth Cavalry of African American soldiers at Fort Riley and station the regiment there permanently? When Junction City's most famous photographer died unexpectedly in April 1922, he left the recording of those next chapters of local history to others. This book must do the same.[162]

Notes

Joseph Judd Pennell and the Era of Commercial Studio Photography, by John Pultz

Many people helped me with this project. I want to thank the staff of the Kansas Collection at the University of Kansas Libraries for aiding my research there, especially Kristin W. Eshelman, who helped in numerous ways not only with material under her care but also by offering her thoughts on Pennell and his work; James Shortridge, who shared his intimate knowledge of Pennell's photographs; Carla Tilghman for her research on Pennell; Jon Blumb for discussing what he had learned from printing Pennell's negatives for this book; David Colemen, curator of photography at the Harry Ransom Humanities Research Center, University of Texas, Austin, for his guidance through archives under his care; and Susan Earle for reading drafts of this essay as it emerged. I am deeply indebted to Nicolette Bromberg, former photo-archivist at the Kansas Collection and now at the State Historical Society of Wisconsin; Thomas Southall, former curator of photography at the Spencer Museum of Art and now in the same position at the High Museum of Art in Atlanta; and Sheryl Williams, Spencer Research Library, for their research undertaken over the past twenty years into the life and work of Joseph Pennell, which formed the basis of the material presented here. Thanks are also due to the Kansas University Art History Department Travel Fund, which supported my travel to the Harry Ransom Center to research commercial studio photographers who were contemporary with Pennell.

1. Beulah Pennell to Frank Aydelotte, December 4, 1970, Joseph Judd Pennell Photograph Collection Accession Files, Kansas Collection, University of Kansas Libraries (hereafter cited as Pennell Files, KC/UKL).

2. Joseph Stanley Pennell, "The Country Photographer," unpublished manuscript, Joseph Stanley Pennell Collection, University of Oregon Libraries. In this unfinished manuscript, the younger Pennell wrote in the fictional voice of his father, a photographer writing his autobiography. The fragment is an evocative, if at times inaccurate, chronicle of the father's beginnings as a photographer. The Junction City address on the manuscript suggests that it was written before the younger Pennell left that city in 1949.

3. "His Splendid Success," *Junction City Sentinel,* October 25, 1901, p. 1.

4. Joseph J. Pennell obituary, *Junction City Republic,* April 6, 1922.

5. Joseph J. Pennell obituary, *Junction City Union,* April 4, 1922.

6. This observation was first suggested by James Shortridge on the basis of his reading of Junction City newspapers from the era and his research into the social and economic standing of Pennell's clients. According to the 1908–1909 city directory, the other photographic studios were Sidney Busby's, at 406½ North Washington, and Louis Teitzel's, at 714 North Washington. The other photographers in town were Robert Kiernan, who worked for Teitzel, Frank Sawtell, who worked for Pennell, and Pennell's former partner, Ed Zellner, who no longer had a business but may have worked from home.

7. Prewitt Directory Company, comp., *Junction City, Kansas, City Directory for 1908–1909* (Springfield, Mo.: Prewitt Directory Company, 1909).

8. "Little Things in Business Methods," *Studio Light,* March 1912, p. 4, quoted in Barbara McCandless, *Equal before the Lens: Jno. Trlica's Photography of Granger, Texas* (College Station: Texas A&M University Press, 1992), p. 21.

9. From the 1922 Junction City High School yearbook: "There is still on file in the superintendent's office an interesting exhibition of pictures of the Junction City schools which was shown at the World's Fair in Chicago in 1891 [*sic*]. This exhibition as well as the one shown at the St. Louis exposition in 1904, was prepared by Mr. Pennell" (Geary County Historical Society).

10. "First Prize Photography, J. J. Pennell's Was Judged Best in State This Week," *Junction City Union,* October 21, 1905.

11. Larry B. Stevens, technical sales representative, Eastman Kodak Company, to Beaumont Newhall, curator, George Eastman House, Rochester, January 26, 1971, Pennell Files, KC/UKL.

12. The social, aesthetic, and economic implications of collodion photography are especially well described in John Szarkowski, *Photography until Now* (New York: Museum of Modern Art, 1989), 125–48.

13. As Robert Taft has noted, the "largest relative increase" in the number of photographers listed in the *U.S. Decennial Census Reports* came in "decades that the new processes were introduced." In the decade between 1880 and 1890, which saw the introduction of dry-plate photography, the number of photographers doubled from 10,000 to 20,000, at a time when the U.S. population increased by 26 percent. Robert Taft, *Photography and the American Scene: A Social History, 1839–1889* (New York: Macmillan, 1938; reprint, New York: Dover, 1964), p. 61 n.

14. Thomas Southall Collection, Atlanta.

15. Joseph Stanley Pennell to Robert Taft, November 8, 1951, Pennell Files, KC/UKL.

16. My thanks for this observation go to Jon Blumb, who printed Pennell's negatives for this book.

17. A portrait of Pennell, dated 1896, has stamped on the back: "From Pennell's Studio/Fine Portraits, Pictures Framed, Kodaks and Finishing, Junction City, Kansas" (Pennell Collection, KC/UKL).

18. This idea was first suggested by Thomas Southall in an unpublished chronology of Pennell's life.

19. Junction City Chamber of Commerce to Margaret Groner, associate curator, Kansas Collection, Spencer Research Library, March 31, 1975, Pennell Files, KC/UKL.

20. On Joseph Stanley Pennell, see his obituary, *Kansas City Times,* September 28, 1963.

21. Joseph Stanley Pennell to Robert Taft, June 20, 1950, Pennell Files, KC/UKL.

22. Taft, *Photography and the American Scene,* p. viii.

23. Sheryl Williams, "Preservation and Cataloguing of the J. J. Pennell Photographic Collection" (report of grant to University of Kansas Libraries, Kansas Collection, by National Endowment for the Humanities, March 20, 1985); and Nicolette Bromberg and John Mark Lambertson, Joseph Judd Pennell Photograph Collection finding aid, Kansas Collection, University of Kansas Libraries, 1985.

24. Pennell broke the photographs into four subject areas: "1—The life of a small Kansas town, from approximately 1880 to 1922. 2—A photographic history of the U.S. Cavalry and allied arms for the same years. 3—Photographs of the topography around Junction City and Fort Riley. 4—Incidental subjects, such as 'prize photographs,' Theodore Roosevelt speaking at the Junction City station and so forth" (Joseph Stanley Pennell to Robert Taft, June 20, 1950, Pennell Files, KC/UKL).

25. Robert Taft to Joseph Stanley Pennell, June 30, 1950, and Joseph Stanley Pennell to Robert Taft, July 22, 1950, Pennell Files, KC/UKL.

26. Louis George Griffin III, curator, Kansas Collection, untitled typescript, Pennell Files, KC/UKL.

Junction City in a Golden Age, 1893–1922

I adapted the street grid for maps 2, 5, 6, and 7 from a fire insurance map prepared for Junction City in 1905 by the Sanborn Map Company of New York City. The same insurance map provides most of the information on the construction, location, and shape of buildings depicted on maps 2 and 3. Additional data on business types and locations for map 3 came from the *1905 Directory of Junction City, Kansas* (n.p.: George C. Peck, 1905). Listings for African American households (map 5) and for railroad employees (map 6) are from the *Junction City, Kansas, City Directory for 1908–1909* (Springfield, Mo.: Prewitt Directory Company, 1909). Memberships in the Junction City Country Club (map 7) are listed in the *Junction City Union* for April 24, 1904, and April 27, 1911. I matched these names with addresses from the 1905 and 1908–1909 city directories. Finally, for map 4, I used as my authority for basic building and street locations a map of the Fort Riley reservation that was prepared in 1919 under the direction of Colonel George H. Cameron. Cameron's map was published in the 1997 reprinting of Woodbury F. Pride's *The History of Fort Riley.*

1. *Junction City Union,* June 16, 1921; October 20, 1921; and October 27, 1921.

2. Richard V. Francaviglia, *Main Street Revisited* (Iowa City: University of Iowa Press, 1996); John A. Jakle, *The American Small Town: Twentieth-Century Place Images* (Hamden, Conn.: Shoe String Press, 1982); John B. Jackson, *The Necessity for Ruins and Other Topics* (Amherst: University of Massachusetts Press, 1980); Leo Marx, *The Machine in the Garden: Technology and the Pastoral Ideal in America* (London: Oxford University Press, 1964).

3. Lewis Atherton, *Main Street on the Middle Border* (Bloomington: Indiana University Press, 1954).

4. Wayne E. Fuller, "Good Roads and Rural Free Delivery of Mail," *Mississippi Valley Historical Review* 42 (1955): 67–83; *Junction City Union,* December 4, 1903, p. 1.

5. William A. Dobak, *Fort Riley and Its Neighbors: Military Money and Economic Growth, 1853–1895* (Norman: University of Oklahoma Press, 1998), p. 11.

6. Ibid., pp. 21–43.

7. Ibid.

8. John B. Jeffries, "An Early History of Junction City, Kansas: The First Generation" (master's thesis, Department of History, Political Science, and Philosophy, Kansas State University, 1963), pp. 12–18; Eugene T. Wells, "St. Louis and Cities West, 1820–1880: A Study in History and Geography" (Ph.D. diss., Department of History, University of Kansas, 1951), pp. 578–96.

9. Dobak, *Fort Riley,* pp. 133–42; Daniel Fitzgerald, *Ghost Towns of Kansas: A Traveler's Guide* (Lawrence: University Press of Kansas, 1988), pp. 39–43; George W. Martin, "The Territorial and Military Combine at Fort Riley," *Kansas Historical Collections* 7 (1901–1902): 361–90; Robert W. Richmond, "The First Capitol of Kansas," *Kansas Historical Quarterly* 21 (1955): 321–25.

10. Jeffries, "An Early History," pp. 20–21; Carolyn Jones, *The First One Hundred Years: A History of the City of Manhattan, Kansas, 1855–1955* (Manhattan, Kans.: Manhattan Centennial, 1955), pp. 11–14; Winifred N. Slagg, *Riley County Kansas: A Story of Early Settlements, Rich Valleys, Azure Skies and Sunflowers* (Manhattan, Kans.: Winifred N. Slagg, 1968), pp. 47–51.

11. Jeffries, "An Early History," pp. 22–23; William G. Cutler, ed., *History of the State of Kansas* (Chicago: A. T. Andreas, 1883), p. 1001.

12. Jeffries, "An Early History," pp. 24–27; Cutler, *History of the State,* p. 1006.

13. George W. Martin recalled this political history in an address at Junction City in 1909. It was printed as an extended footnote to Theodore Weichselbaum's "Statement of Theodore Weichselbaum, of Ogden, Riley County, July 17, 1908," *Kansas Historical Collections* 11 (1909–1910): 561–63.

14. William R. Petrowski, *The Kansas Pacific: A Study in Railroad Promotion* (New York: Arno Press, 1981), pp. 48–141; Dobak, *Fort Riley,* p. 59; Jeffries, "An Early History," pp. 55–63, 130–33.

15. Petrowski, *The Kansas Pacific,* pp. 142–50.

16. Ibid.

17. Dobak, *Fort Riley,* pp. 68, 132–33, 142–48.

18. Jeffries, "An Early History," pp. 64–75; Dobak, *Fort Riley,* pp. 89–111.

19. Ibid.

20. Joseph G. McCoy, *Historic Sketches of the Cattle Trade of the West and Southwest* (Glendale, Calif.: A. H. Clark, 1940), p. 113; Jeffries, "An Early History," p. 157.

21. Jeffries, "An Early History," pp. 132, 145; Dobak, *Fort Riley,* p. 101.

22. Dobak, *Fort Riley,* pp. 120, 127–30.

23. Ibid., pp. 111, 123–27.

24. Ibid., pp. 157, 165.

25. Ibid., pp. 171–75.

26. Ibid., p. 11.

27. Francaviglia, *Main Street Revisited,* p. xviii.

28. *Junction City Union,* December 22, 1894.

29. Gaylynn Childs, "York Family Known for Long Tradition of Stone Mason Skill," *Junction City Union,* August 31, 1986; *Junction City Union,* January 3, 1902.

30. *Junction City Union,* August 18, 1905; September 15, 1905.

31. A brief history of the Ziegler and Dalton form appears in the *Junction City Union,* April 10, 1913. More details are in Frank Z. Glick's family account, *They Came to the Smoky Hill: History of Three Generations* (Manhattan, Kans.: Sunflower University Press, 1987), pp. 36–39, 100–105, 270–72. The Ziegler and Dalton company mentioned at the beginning of this essay was a different but related group comprising two sons of Charley Ziegler and one of John Dalton.

32. *Junction City Union,* September 29, 1905.

33. Susan L. Franzen, *Behind the Facade of Fort Riley's Hometown* (Ames, Iowa: Pivot Press, 1998), pp. 48–51.

34. *Junction City Union,* February 22, 1896.

35. Ibid., June 16, 1899; Arman J. Habegger, "Out of the Mud: The Good Roads Movement in Kansas, 1900–1917" (master's thesis, Department of History, University of Kansas, 1971), pp. 107–12. See also Ira O. Baker, *A Treatise of Roads and Pavements* (New York: John Wiley and Sons, 1914).

36. Atherton, *Main Street,* p. 149.

37. *Junction City Union,* July 26, 1901; August 2, 1901.

38. Franzen, *Behind the Facade,* p. 44.

39. Loren Reid, *Hurry Home Wednesday: Growing up in a Small Missouri Town, 1905–1921* (Columbia: University of Missouri Press, 1978), p. 19.

40. *Junction City Union,* March 19, 1897.

41. Reid, *Hurry Home Wednesday,* p. 122.

42. Ibid.

43. *Junction City Union,* June 2, 1899.

44. Frederick F. DeArmond, *The Laundry Industry* (New York: Harper and Brothers, 1950), p. 32.

45. *Junction City Union,* August 11, 1899.

46. Ibid., September 6, 1901.

47. Glick, *They Came to the Smoky Hill,* pp. 64–65.

48. The volume of these products from hundreds of small farmers is impressive. The *Union* reported a record week on March 23, 1900, when 3,750 dozen eggs were brought into town to sell.

49. *Junction City Union,* February 2, 1895.

50. Ibid., January 19, 1900; March 16, 1900.

51. Ibid., September 29, 1905.

52. Ibid., October 1, 1909.

53. Ibid., May 5, 1899.

54. Glick, *They Came to the Smoky Hill,* p. 264; *Junction City Union,* May 19, 1899; June 8, 1899.

55. *Junction City Union,* June 2, 1899.

56. Michael K. Witzel and Gyvel Young-Witzel, *Soda Pop! From Miracle Medicine to Pop Culture* (Stillwater, Minn.: Voyageur Press, 1998), pp. 39–40; *Junction City Union,* March 25, 1898.

57. *Junction City Union,* September 20, 1907; February 24, 1916.

58. Ibid., January 29, 1904.

59. Ibid., January 5, 1895; February 28, 1908.

60. Ibid., September 23, 1920.

61. *Topeka Plaindealer,* January 18, 1918.

62. Joan Severa, *Dressed for the Photographer: Ordinary Americans and Fashions, 1840–1900* (Kent, Ohio: Kent State University Press, 1995), pp. 454–74; *The 1902 Edition of the Sears Roebuck Catalog* (New York: Crown Publishers, 1969).

63. *Junction City Union,* March 25, 1915.

64. Ibid., June 17, 1915.

65. Ibid., March 30, 1895; May 26, 1899; December 16, 1904.

66. Jeffries, "An Early History," pp. 113–14.

67. Ibid., p. 108.

68. *Topeka Commonwealth,* July 27, 1884.

69. Franzen, *Behind the Facade,* p. 149; *Junction City Union,* February 29, 1896.

70. *Junction City Union,* November 24, 1899; April 29, 1955.

71. George W. Martin, "Thomas Allen Cullinan of Junction City," *Kansas Historical Collections* 9 (1905–1906): 532–40. An obituary is in the *Junction City Union,* June 24, 1904.

72. Martin, "Thomas Allen Cullinan," p. 538.

73. *Junction City Union,* February 22, 1901.

74. A page-one story entitled "Don't Want Negro Cavalry" appeared in the *Union* on July 22, 1904. Although ostensibly about a similar situation in Leavenworth, the context makes it clear that the sentiment was also held locally. A racial incident involving soldiers from the Ninth Cavalry was reported in the issue of August 26, 1904.

75. *Junction City Union,* November 23 and 30, 1906. Local ramifications are reported in the issues of January 11 and February 22, 1907.

76. Ibid., October 25, 1907.

77. Ibid., September 2, 1904.

78. A firsthand account of cooking for threshers is in Carrie Young, *Nothing to Do but Stay: My Prairie Mother* (Iowa City: University of Iowa Press, 1991), pp. 69–86. Many crews furnished their own cooks and cook wagons to spare the farmwives.

79. *Junction City Union,* September 8, 1899.

80. Ibid., September 17, 1909; September 24, 1909.

81. Ibid., August 24, 1911; September 16, 1915.

82. Ibid., January 13, 1899; September 8, 1899; June 1, 1900.

83. Ibid., September 2, 1898; July 20, 1900; January 20, 1904; June 4, 1909.

84. Ibid., September 5, 1902; July 28, 1905; May 9, 1906.

85. *Junction City Tribune,* October 17, 1889; *Junction City Union,* March 16, 1889; December 21, 1895.

86. *Topeka Daily Capital,* December 24, 1907; *Junction City Union,* July 5, 1907; October 11, 1907; November 6, 1908; July 1, 1910; September 6, 1917.

87. *Junction City Union,* December 21, 1895; September 18, 1919.

88. Woodbury F. Pride, *The History of Fort Riley* (Topeka, Kans.: Capper, 1926), pp. 194–213; *Junction City Union,* September 4, 1896; *Kansas City Journal,* March 2, 1902.

89. Dobak, *Fort Riley,* pp. 160–64.

90. Pride, *History of Fort Riley,* pp. 193–213.

91. *Junction City Union,* March 27, 1907.

92. Lucian K. Truscott, Jr., *The Twilight of the U.S. Cavalry: Life in the Old Army, 1917–1942* (Lawrence: University Press of Kansas, 1989), p. xix.

93. Reprinted in the *Junction City Union,* March 4, 1900.

94. Truscott, *Twilight,* pp. 117–18; Pride, *History of Fort Riley,* p. 255; *Junction City Union,* August 31, 1906; January 15, 1914.

95. Truscott, *Twilight,* pp. viii, 38, 53; Pride, *History of Fort Riley,* p. 255.

96. Truscott, *Twilight,* p. 78.

97. Ibid., pp. xv–xvi. The father was Lucian K. Truscott, Jr., the son Lucian K. Truscott III.

98. Pride, *History of Fort Riley,* p. 207; Truscott, *Twilight,* pp. 97–100.

99. *Junction City Union,* August 23, 1901. Joseph Stanley Pennell, the photographer's son, makes reference to these meetings in his fictionalized account of local life: *The History of Nora Beck-*

ham: A Museum of Home Life (New York: Charles Scribner's Sons, 1948), p. 206.

100. Gaylynn Childs, "Life during Turn-of-the-Century Fort Riley," *Junction City Union,* July 24, 1988. See also Truscott, *Twilight,* pp. 85–87.

101. *Junction City Union,* December 14, 1895; September 30, 1898; March 1, 1900; July 10, 1903.

102. Pennell, *Nora Beckham,* pp. 106–7.

103. *Junction City Union,* August 31, 1895.

104. Franzen, *Behind the Facade,* p. 131; Pennell, *Nora Beckham,* pp. 34–35, 292.

105. Prewitt Directory Company, comp., *Junction City, Kansas, City Directory for 1908–1909* (Springfield, Mo.: Prewitt Directory Company, 1909).

106. *Junction City Union,* October 24, 1942.

107. Atherton, *Main Street,* p. 84.

108. Cutler, *History of the State,* p. 1007; Atherton, *Main Street,* pp. 117–18, 135–42.

109. *Junction City Union,* October 31, 1898.

110. Glick, *They Came to the Smoky Hill,* p. 105; *Junction City Union,* April 14, 1899.

111. *Junction City Union,* April 21, 1899; May 5, 1899.

112. Ibid., May 12, 1899; August 24, 1900; March 13, 1903.

113. Ibid., April 10, 1903; Helen H. Santmyer, *". . . And Ladies of the Club"* (Columbus: Ohio State University Press, 1982), pp. 926–29.

114. *Junction City Union,* January 13, 1905; June 15, 1906. Smith's decision may have been influenced by an earlier editorial that had called for a businessman to endow a library as a legacy to the community. See *Junction City Union,* May 19, 1899.

115. Ibid., September 10, 1897; November 5, 1897; April 1, 1898; September 16, 1898.

116. Franzen, *Behind the Facade,* p. 68; see also Jacob V. Brower, *Quivira* (Saint Paul, Minn.: H. L. Collins, 1898), and W. E. Richey, "The Real Quivira," *Kansas Historical Collections* 6 (1897–1900): 477–85.

117. Scott Bruce and Bill Crawford, *Cerealizing America: The Unsweetened Story of American Breakfast Cereal* (Boston: Faber and Faber, 1995), pp. 27–30.

118. *Junction City Union,* March 27, 1913; March 18, 1915.

119. Harold C. Evans, "Baseball in Kansas, 1867–1940," *Kansas Historical Quarterly* 9 (1940): 175–77; *Junction City Union,* December 28, 1895.

120. *Junction City Union,* May 30, 1896.

121. Ibid., July 25, 1912; August 1, 1912; August 22, 1912.

122. Gaylynn Childs, "Upcoming Concert Prompts Much Activity at Museum," *Junction City Union,* March 15, 1987.

123. *City Directory for 1908–1909,* pp. 10–11.

124. *Junction City Union,* May 6, 1910. See also the issues of May 3, 1901; April 29, 1904; and the special centennial one dated June 1961.

125. Marilyn I. Holt, *Linoleum, Better Babies and the Modern Farm Woman, 1890–1930* (Albuquerque: University of New Mexico Press, 1995), pp. 18–91; *Junction City Union,* February 9, 1900.

126. Marilyn D. Brady, "Kansas Federation of Colored Women's Clubs, 1900–1930," *Kansas History* 9 (1986): 19–30; June C. Underwood, "Civilizing Kansas: Women's Organizations, 1880–1920," *Kansas History* 7 (1984): 291–306.

127. *Junction City Union,* May 30, 1902.

128. Ibid., July 11, 1902.

129. Ibid., August 18, 1905; September 15, 1905.

130. Ibid., March 30, 1903; April 17, 1903; April 24, 1903; May 1, 1903; May 8, 1903.

131. Ibid., June 5, 1903. See also the issues of May 15, 1903; May 29, 1903; and June 3, 1904. For statewide coverage, see the *Kansas City Star,* May 30, 1903.

132. Edmund G. Love, *The Situation in Flushing* (New York: Harper and Row, 1965), p. 1.

133. *Junction City Union,* August 10, 1900; April 14, 1996.

134. Ibid., February 22, 1896; April 21, 1899; August 3, 1906.

135. Ibid., October 8, 1897; February 4, 1898; January 3, 1902, March 26, 1914.

136. Ibid., August 16, 1901.

137. Ibid.

138. Ibid., August 16, 1901; September 20, 1901; Allison Chandler, *Trolley through the Countryside* (Denver: Sage Books, 1963), pp. 102–28. The initial car barn was on East Eighth Street (see map 2). It was moved sometime before 1905. At Fort Riley, the company extended the line a mile beyond Waters Hall in 1906, where in 1914 it made a connection with another trolley system that originated in Manhattan.

139. *Junction City Union,* October 1, 1897; September 1, 1899; December 22, 1899.

140. Ibid., June 8, 1900; January 11, 1901; October 19, 1906.

141. Ibid., September 2, 1893; February 29, 1896; July 10, 1896; January 6, 1899.

142. Severa, *Dressed for the Photographer,* p. 455; Dorothy W. Regur, "In the Bicycle Era," *Palimpsest* 14 (1933): 349–62; Jay Pridmont and Jim Hurd, *The American Bicycle* (Osceola, Wis.: Motorbooks International, 1995).

143. John B. Rae, *The Road and the Car in American Life* (Cambridge, Mass.: MIT Press, 1971), p. 8; *Junction City Union,* April 21, 1899.

144. *Junction City Union,* March 10, 1905; March 31, 1905.

145. Ibid., April 7, 1905; July 28, 1905; September 15, 1905.

146. Ibid., July 7, 1905; December 1, 1905.

147. Ibid., August 25, 1905.

148. Ibid., February 16, 1906; February 23, 1906.

149. Ibid., August 16, 1907; September 13, 1907.

150. Pennell, *Nora Beckham,* p. 7; Santmyer, *Ladies of the Club,* p. 1114. Richer women had another option beyond the family horse and carriage. Electric cars came on the market and soon were perceived and sold almost exclusively as women's vehicles (*Junction City Union,* November 30, 1916; January 20, 1921).

151. *Junction City Union,* January 6, 1905; January 13, 1905; January 20, 1905; January 27, 1905; April 17, 1908; May 29, 1908; July 3, 1908; September 11, 1908; August 6, 1909; December 14, 1911; Habegger, "Out of the Mud," pp. 106–88.

152. *Junction City Union,* February 11, 1910; March 26, 1914; December 10, 1914; May 31, 1917; May 22, 1919.

153. Ibid., May 17, 1917; May 24, 1917; June 28, 1917; August 23, 1917.

154. Ibid., June 7, 1917; June 21, 1917; June 28, 1917; July 5, 1917; August 9, 1917; *Topeka Daily Capital,* May 15, 1917.

155. Ibid., July 5, 1917; September 6, 1917.

156. Ibid., December 19, 1912; February 26, 1914; *Junction City Republic,* special industrial issue dated July 1915. Terra-cotta tile was used most extensively at the time for Spanish mission decor. An early local example was the hospital, constructed in 1920–1921 at the south end of Jefferson Street.

157. *Junction City Union,* September 17, 1914; September 20, 1917.

158. Ibid., September 10, 1909.

159. Ibid., August 16, 1917; October 4, 1917; March 7, 1918; November 28, 1918.

160. *Junction City Republic,* special women's edition, 1895, as quoted in Gaylynn Childs, "'Mother Hubbard' Dress Raises Editor's Ire," *Junction City Republic,* March 16, 1986.

161. *Junction City Union,* October 16, 1908. See also JoAnne Olian, ed., *Everyday Fashions, 1909–1920, as Pictured in Sears Catalogs* (New York: Dover Publications, 1995), pp. 3–4.

162. *Junction City Union,* December 23, 1915; August 24, 1922; October 5, 1922; November 2, 1922; November 16, 1922.

Bibliography

Adams, Franklin G., comp. *The Homestead Guide.* Waterville, Kans.: F. G. Adams, 1873.

Ames, Kenneth L. "Material Culture as Non-Verbal Communication." *Journal of American Culture* 3 (1980): 619–41.

Atherton, Lewis. *Main Street on the Middle Border.* Bloomington: Indiana University Press, 1954.

Bader, Robert S. *Prohibition in Kansas: A History.* Lawrence: University Press of Kansas, 1986.

Baker, Ira O. *A Treatise on Roads and Pavements.* New York: John Wiley and Sons, 1914.

Bastian, Robert W. "Architecture and Class Segregation in Late Nineteenth-Century Terre Haute, Indiana." *Geographical Review* 65 (1975): 166–79.

Benton, Thomas H. *An Artist in America.* 3d ed., rev. Columbia: University of Missouri Press, 1968.

Bolton, Kate. "The Great Awakening of the Night: Lighting America's Streets." *Landscape* 23, no. 3 (1979): 41–47.

Brady, Marilyn D. "Kansas Federation of Colored Women's Clubs, 1900–1930." *Kansas History* 9 (1986): 19–30.

Brower, Jacob V. *Quivira.* Saint Paul, Minn.: H. L. Collins, 1898.

Bruce, Scott, and Bill Crawford. *Cerealizing America: The Unsweetened Story of American Breakfast Cereal.* Boston: Faber and Faber, 1995.

Campbell, Karolyn K., Deborah Dandridge, and Marilyn D. Brady. *Afro-American Clubwomen in Kansas: Achievements against the Odds.* Lawrence: Women's Studies Program, University of Kansas, 1985.

Carroll, John M., ed. *The Black Military Experience in the American West.* New York: Liveright, 1971.

"The Cavalry Post of Fort Riley Kansas." *Journal of the U.S. Cavalry Association* 13 (October 1902): 113–29.

Chandler, Allison. *Trolley through the Countryside.* Denver: Sage Books, 1963.

Childs, Gaylynn. "Junction City Pool Was a Favorite Cool Spot." *Junction City Union,* July 14, 1985.

———. "Museum Display Features 'Night at the Opera House.'" *Junction City Union,* December 22, 1985.

———. "'Mother Hubbard' Dress Raises Editor's Ire." *Junction City Republic,* March 16, 1986.

———. "York Family Known for Long Tradition of Stone Mason Skill," *Junction City Union,* August 31, 1986.

———. "Upcoming Concert Prompts Much Activity at Museum." *Junction City Union,* March 15, 1987.

———. "Life during Turn-of-the-Century Fort Riley." *Junction City Union,* July 24, 1988.

———. "Bicycling Hit Junction City in the Late 1890s." *Junction City Union,* July 8, 1990.

———. "Over 82 Years, Three City Pools." *Junction City Union,* June 18, 1995.

Cochran, Thomas C. *Pabst Brewing Company: The History of an American Business.* New York: New York University Press, 1948.

Corle, Edwin. *John Studebaker: An American Dream.* New York: E. P. Dutton, 1948.

Crabb, Richard. *Birth of a Giant.* New York: Chilton Book Co., 1969.

Cutler, William G., ed. *History of the State of Kansas.* Chicago: A. T. Andreas, 1883.

Davis-Geary County clippings, 1876–date. 6 vols. Kansas State Historical Society, Topeka.

DeArmond, Frederick F. *The Laundry Industry.* New York: Harper and Brothers, 1950.

Dobak, William A. *Fort Riley and Its Neighbors: Military Money and Economic Growth, 1853–1895.* Norman: University of Oklahoma Press, 1998.

Eastman, Philip. "The Fort Riley Maneuvers." *American Monthly Review of Reviews* 28 (November 1903): 564–69.

Ehernberger, James L., and Francis G. Gschwind. *Smoke above the Plains: Union Pacific, Kansas Division.* Callaway, Nebr.: E & G Publications, 1965.

Eliot, Ellsworth, Jr. "Making Medical Officers out of Doctors: Life at the Fort Riley Training Camp." *Outlook* 119 (May 29, 1918): 190–91.

Erskine, Albert R. *History of the Studebaker Corporation.* South Bend, Ind.: Studebaker Corporation, 1924.

Evans, Harold C. "Baseball in Kansas, 1867–1940." *Kansas Historical Quarterly* 9 (1940): 175–92.

Fitzgerald, Daniel. *Ghost Towns of Kansas: A Traveler's Guide.* Lawrence: University Press of Kansas, 1988.

Fletcher, Marvin. *The Black Soldier and Officer in the United States Army, 1891–1917.* Columbia: University of Missouri Press, 1974.

Fontenot, Gregory. "Junction City–Fort Riley: A Case of Symbiosis." In *The Martial Metropolis: U.S. Cities in War and Peace,* ed. Roger W. Lotchin, pp. 35–60. New York: Praeger, 1984.

Fort Riley clippings, 1855–date. 5 vols. Kansas State Historical Society, Topeka.

Francaviglia, Richard V. *Main Street Revisited.* Iowa City: University of Iowa Press, 1996.

Franzen, Susan L. *Behind the Facade of Fort Riley's Hometown.* Ames, Iowa: Pivot Press, 1998.

Fuller, Wayne E. "Good Roads and Rural Free Delivery of Mail." *Mississippi Valley Historical Review* 42 (1955): 67–83.

George, Kathy B., and Ralph Murphy. "Music Evolves in Junction City." *Junction City Republic,* November 13, 1983.

———. "Muenzenmayers Give Legacy." *Junction City Republic,* August 29, 1984.

Glick, Frank Z. *They Came to the Smoky Hill: History of Three Generations.* Manhattan, Kans.: Sunflower University Press, 1987.

Gowans, Alan. *Images of American Living: Four Centuries of Architecture and Furniture as Cultural Expression.* Philadelphia: J. B. Lippincott, 1964.

Gray, R. B. *The American Farm Tractor: 1855–1950.* Saint Joseph, Mo.: American Society of Agricultural Engineers, 1975.

Habegger, Arman J. "Out of the Mud: The Good Roads Movement in Kansas, 1900–1917." Master's thesis, Department of History, University of Kansas, 1971.

Heldstab, Marilyn. "Junction City Home to Celebrate 100th Birthday." *Junction City Union,* September 12, 1993.

Holt, Marilyn I. *Linoleum, Better Babies and the Modern Farm Woman, 1890–1930.* Albuquerque: University of New Mexico Press, 1995.

Hoy, Suellen. *Chasing Dirt: The American Pursuit of Cleanliness.* New York: Oxford University Press, 1995.

Humphrey, James. "The Country West of Topeka Prior to 1865." *Kansas Historical Collections* 4 (1886–1890): 289–97.

Isern, Thomas D. *Bull Threshers and Bindlestiffs: Harvesting and Threshing on the North American Plains.* Lawrence: University Press of Kansas, 1990.

Jackson, John B. *The Necessity for Ruins and Other Topics.* Amherst: University of Massachusetts Press, 1980.

Jakle, John A. *The American Small Town: Twentieth-Century Place Images.* Hamden, Conn.: Shoe String Press, 1982.

Jakle, John A., Robert W. Bastian, and Douglas K. Meyer. *Common Houses in America's Small Towns: The Atlantic Seaboard to the Mississippi Valley.* Athens: University of Georgia Press, 1989.

Jakle, John A., and Keith A. Sculle. *The Gas Station in America.* Baltimore: Johns Hopkins University Press, 1994.

Jeffries, John B. "An Early History of Junction City, Kansas: The First Generation." Master's thesis, Department of History, Political Science, and Philosophy, Kansas State University, 1963.

Jeffries, John B., and Irene Jeffries, comps. and eds. *Garden of Eden: A Pictorial History of Geary County Kansas.* Junction City, Kans.: Geary County Historical Society, 1978.

Jones, Carolyn. *The First One Hundred Years: A History of the City of Manhattan, Kansas, 1855–1955.* Manhattan, Kans.: Manhattan Centennial, 1955.

Josselyn, Homer W. "Survey of Accredited High Schools and Professional Directory." *Bulletin of the University of Kansas* 15, no. 16 (1914).

Kowalke, Ron, ed. *Standard Catalogue of Ford: 1903–1998.* Iola, Wis.: Krause Publishing, 1998.

Leckie, William H. *The Buffalo Soldiers: A Narrative of the Negro Cavalry in the West.* Norman: University of Oklahoma Press, 1967.

Lesy, Michael. *Wisconsin Death Trip.* New York: Pantheon Books, 1973.

Lewis, Sinclair. *Main Street: The Story of Carol Kennicott.* New York: Harcourt, Brace, 1920.

Love, Edmund G. *The Situation in Flushing.* New York: Harper and Row, 1965.
Lowe, Percival G. "Recollections of Fort Riley." *Kansas Historical Collections* 7 (1901–1902): 101–13.
Makins, A. E. "Fort Riley—Cavalry Hub of the Nation." *Kansas Business Magazine* 9 (December 1941): 12, 26–27.
Martin, George W. "The Territorial and Military Combine at Fort Riley." *Kansas Historical Collections* 7 (1901–1902): 361–90.
———. "Thomas Allen Cullinan, of Junction City." *Kansas Historical Collections* 9 (1905–1906): 532–40.
Marx, Leo. *The Machine in the Garden: Technology and the Pastoral Ideal in America.* London: Oxford University Press, 1964.
McConnell, Curt. *Great Cars of the Great Plains.* Lincoln: University of Nebraska Press, 1995.
McCoy, Joseph G. *Historic Sketches of the Cattle Trade of the West and Southwest.* Glendale, Calif.: A. H. Clark, 1940.
Mounted Service School, Fort Riley, Kansas. Fort Riley: Mounted Service School, 1916.
The 1902 Edition of the Sears Roebuck Catalog. New York: Crown Publishers, 1969.
Olian, JoAnne, ed. *Everyday Fashions, 1909–1920, as Pictured in Sears Catalogs.* New York: Dover Publications, 1995.
Olney, Elaine W., and Mary F. J. Roberts, coords. *Pioneers of the Bluestem Prairie.* Manhattan, Kans.: Riley County Genealogical Society, 1976.
Peck, George C. *1905 Directory of Junction City, Kansas.* N.p.: George C. Peck, 1905.
Pennell, J. J., and C. S. McGirr. *Picturesque Fort Riley in Photo-Gravure from Recent Negatives.* Junction City, Kans.: Pennell and McGirr, 1900.
Pennell, Joseph S. *The History of Rome Hanks and Kindred Matters.* New York: Charles Scribner's Sons, 1944.
———. *The History of Nora Beckham: A Museum of Home Life.* New York: Charles Scribner's Sons, 1948.
Petrowski, William R. *The Kansas Pacific: A Study in Railroad Promotion.* New York: Arno Press, 1981.
Prewitt Directory Company, comp. *Junction City, Kansas, City Directory for 1908–1909.* Springfield, Mo.: Prewitt Directory Company, 1909.
———. *Junction City, Kansas, City Directory for 1916–1917.* Springfield, Mo.: Prewitt Directory Company, 1917.
Pride, Woodbury F. *The History of Fort Riley.* Topeka, Kans.: Capper, 1926.
Pridmont, Jay, and Jim Hurd. *The American Bicycle.* Osceola, Wis.: Motorbooks International, 1995.
Rae, John B. *The Road and the Car in American Life.* Cambridge, Mass.: MIT Press, 1971.
Regur, Dorothy W. "In the Bicycle Era." *Palimpsest* 14 (1933): 349–62.
Reid, Loren. *Hurry Home Wednesday: Growing up in a Small Missouri Town, 1905–1921.* Columbia: University of Missouri Press, 1978.
Richey, W. E. "The Real Quivira." *Kansas Historical Collections* 6 (1897–1900): 477–85.
Richmond, Robert W. "The First Capitol of Kansas." *Kansas Historical Quarterly* 21 (1955): 321–25.
Rion, George P. "Army City, Kansas: The History of a World War I Camptown." Master's thesis, Department of History, Political Science, and Philosophy, Kansas State University, 1960.
Rybczynski, Witold. *Home: A Short History of an Idea.* New York: Viking Press, 1986.
Sanborn Map Company. Fire insurance maps for Junction City for 1885, 1887, 1892, 1897, 1905, 1912, and 1925. New York: Sanborn Map Company.
Santmyer, Helen H. *Ohio Town.* Columbus: Ohio State University Press, 1963.
———. "*. . . And Ladies of the Club.*" Columbus: Ohio State University Press, 1982.
Severa, Joan. *Dressed for the Photographer: Ordinary Americans and Fashions, 1840–1900.* Kent, Ohio: Kent State University Press, 1995.
Slagg, Winifred N. *Riley County Kansas: A Story of Early Settlements, Rich Valleys, Azure Skies and Sunflowers.* Manhattan, Kans.: Winifred N. Slagg, 1968.
Southwick, C. A., and S. P. Essex. *First Annual Junction City, Kas., City Directory.* Junction City, Kans.: C. A. Southwick, 1887.
Suckow, Ruth. *Iowa Interiors.* New York: Alfred Knopf, 1926.
———. "Middle Western Literature." *English Journal* 21 (1932): 175–82.
———. *The Folks.* New York: Farrar and Rinehart, 1934.
"They're Playing Our Song: Community Bands in Kansas." Unpublished script for a museum exhibition. Kansas State Historical Society, Topeka, 1997.
Truscott, Lucian K., Jr. *The Twilight of the U.S. Cavalry: Life in the Old Army, 1917–1942.* Lawrence: University Press of Kansas, 1989.

Twain, Mark. *Mark Twain's Autobiography.* 2 vols. New York: Harper and Brothers, 1924.
Underwood, June C. "Civilizing Kansas: Women's Organizations, 1880–1920." *Kansas History* 7 (1984): 291–306.
Volkman, Nancy J. "Landscape Architecture on the Prairie: The Work of H. W. S. Cleveland." *Kansas History* 10 (1987): 89–110.
von Leeuwen, Thomas A. P. *The Springboard in the Pond: An Intimate History of the Swimming Pool.* Cambridge, Mass.: MIT Press, 1998.
Weichselbaum, Theodore. "Statement of Theodore Weichselbaum of Ogden, Riley County, July 17, 1908." *Kansas Historical Collections* 11 (1909–1910): 561–71.
Wells, Eugene T. "St. Louis and Cities West, 1820–1880: A Study in History and Geography." Ph.D. diss., Department of History, University of Kansas, 1951.
Whiffen, Marcus. *American Architecture since 1780: A Guide to the Styles.* Cambridge, Mass.: MIT Press, 1969.
White, William A. *The Autobiography of William Allen White.* New York: Macmillan, 1946.
Williams, Marilyn T. *Washing "The Great Unwashed": Public Baths in Urban America, 1840–1920.* Columbus: Ohio State University Press, 1991.
Winkler, Gail C., and Roger W. Moss. *Victorian Interior Decoration: American Interiors, 1830–1900.* New York: Henry Holt, 1986.
Witzel, Michael K., and Gyvel Young-Witzel. *Soda Pop! From Miracle Medicine to Pop Culture.* Stillwater, Minn.: Voyageur Press, 1998.
Worley, E. D. *Iron Horses of the Santa Fe Trail.* Dallas: Southwest Railroad Historical Society, 1965.
Wright, Gwendolyn. *Building the Dream: A Social History of Housing in America.* New York: Pantheon Books, 1981.
Young, Carrie. *Nothing to Do but Stay: My Prairie Mother.* Iowa City: University of Iowa Press, 1991.
Young, James H. *The Toadstool Millionaires: A Social History of Patent Medicines in America before Federal Regulation.* Princeton, N.J.: Princeton University Press, 1961.

Index